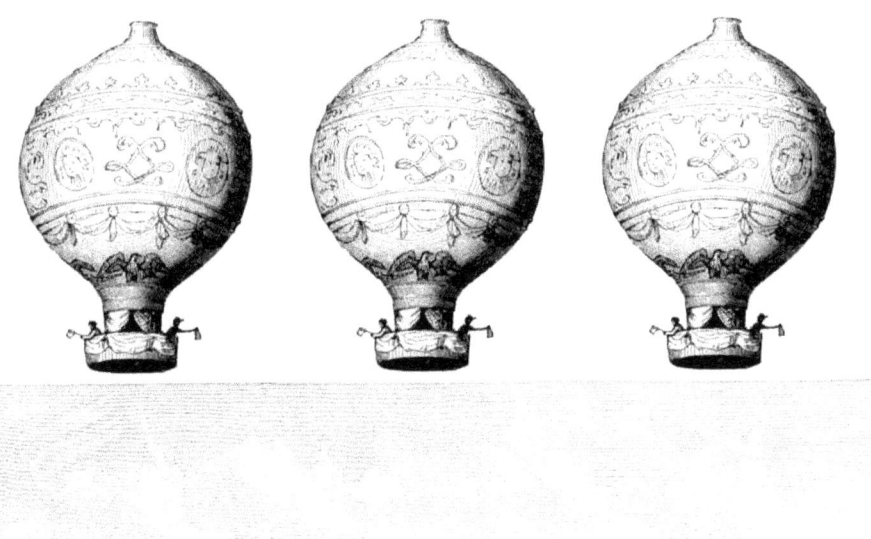

PARADISE GLOSSED

The rants and ramblings of a Bristolian cynic

DARREN HURLEY

First published by Darren Hurley in association with Tangent Books in 2010
Copyright © Darren Hurley 2010

The right of Darren Hurley to be identified as the author of this work has been asserted by him in accordance with the Copyright, Designs and Patents Act, 1988.

All rights reserved. No part of this book may be reproduced in any form or by any electronic or mechanical means, including information storage and retrieval systems, without written permission from the publisher or author, except in the case of a reviewer, who may quote brief passages embodied in critical articles or in a review.

Copyright text: Darren Hurley

Cover design by the author in collaboration with lulu.com.

Printed and bound by Lulu in 2010.

ISBN: 978-0-9566263-0-1

Every effort has been made to acknowledge the appropriate copyright holders.

Acknowledgement to all known authors of copyright-free images are listed at the back of this book.

Contact author at darrenhurley27@talktalk.net

For Mum and Dad, Laura,

and everyone who has encouraged me....

Many thanks to Richard Jones of Tangent Books

FORWARD

"I thought I'd keep a diary thing
of sarcasm and wit -
my humble verses represent
the world from where I sit

Now subjects that I write on,
the ideas are but my own -
I see the world outside my window,
thus, the seeds are sewn

I'm just a normal Bristol bloke
who, like my fellow local folk
has much to say about his town
and those who run the country down

The thing I really cannot take
is everybody's *"on the make"* -
to make a speedy profit's rife
in EVERY aspect of our life

Some people call me cynical
and they accuse me thus -
"Your moaning's reached a pinnacle -
now don't cause such a fuss!"

But can I be the only one
who sees what's going on?
Who looks below the surface
and who sees financial con?

Now the Poets i admire most
are Chesterton and Hood -
'cuz (laced with little bits of Lear),
they make my head feel good

Of English rhyming writers all,
these are the three I'd pick -
because their styles often are
the ones I like to nick.....

With that in mind, I had a funny year
and kept a log -
in which I wrote down all my thoughts
(in rhyme), was quite a slog!

So *this* is it, my anger all let loose -
it isn't good -
yet kinda watered down
it's like a sarcy Thomas Hood!

in short, I ain't no 'Laureatte" -
I'm Bristol's "Poet Borry-it"!

Contents　　　　Turn to Page..........

1. "The Good old Days"..1
2. "Three cheers for Mr Colston"..5
3. "Our Noble Family (Or 'An address to Queen Bess')"................7
4. "Our Noble Leader (Or 'An address to Mr Brown')".................11
5. "The Celebrity Chef"...15
6. "26/5/1999 (two minutes of torture)".....................................16
7. "The world's a giant car-park"..18
8. "Twentieth Century Britain (Part One)".................................19
9. "The man in the stove-pipe hat"..23
10. "Paradise Glossed (Or 'Bush and Blair, the Glory Years')"......26
11. "The Asda Trilogy (Parts One, Two and Three)"....................33
12. "25/5/2005 (six minutes of ecstacy)".....................................35
13. "If I was born in 1937"..37
14. "The Politician who told the truth".......................................39
15. "Twentieth Century Britain (Part Two)"...............................46
16. "Three cheers for Mr Plimsoll"..49
17. "B.I.G. B.A.L.L.s (Or, 'The Great Balloon Hunt')"..................51
18. "Local news is rubbish"...62
19. "I am a child of Thatcher"...64
20. "Evolution of the telephone"...66

21. "The Scotsman's day out in Bristol"......................................68

22. "Twentieth Century Britain (Part Three)"...........................73

23. "Ode to Autumn"..76

24. "PC Cobb (Who had a hard job)"..77

25. "Accents, according to the media"......................................82

26. "The Daily Redtop"..83

27. "The Spirit of Women's Rights"...86

28. "Deals on meals"..88

29. "Loud ugly chap"..89

30. "Paper Man"..90

31. "The Zzzz Factor"..92

32. "Early Morning"...95

33. "The Tenth Doctor Who"..96

34. "Doctor Blinker"..98

35. "Twentieth Century Britain (Part Four)"........................101

36. "Ode to Winter"...104

37. "Three cheers for Mr Cabot"...106

(The Trilogy of Classics)

38. "Peeps Diary, 1660-1669 (Fragments) – by Sammy Peeps"...............108

39. "Manifesto of le comedie Party – (by C Marks and F Angels, 1848)"..114

40. "On the Origin of Beasties – (by Charlie Darwen, 1859)".......................117

41.	"Leaders of Labour"	120
42.	"Three cheers for Billy Wedlock"	122
43.	"A text message"	124
44.	"The Cynic's Calender"	125
45.	"Holly"	127
46.	"TV scams of the 21st Century"	128
47.	"I blame the Government!"	133
48.	"A five-point Manifesto (AKA 'A Personal Pipe-dream')"	135
49.	"The ticking clock"	141
50.	"Ode to the Sun"	142
51.	"Ode to the Moon"	143
52.	"Twentieth Century Britain (Part Five)"	144
53.	"All on April Fool's Day"	146
54.	"C.A.T.A.S.T.R.O.P.H.E."	140
55.	"A week to go before the Election"	152
56.	"Famous last thoughts (?)"	155

"The good old Days"   Friday May 1st 2009

"Finding joy in present days a total mystery?
Then make yourself feel better, take a look at history".........

When William conquered England
(bringing half his Normans too)
we had a "*Bastard*" French asylum-seeker
as our King anew
We lost all of our traditions
and we had to speak in French,
had our castles taken from us -
oh, it did cause such a stench
Now why do current Englishmen
think life is such a wrench?

The Twelfth Century in England -
oh, ye time of little fun
with the Scottish through the borders
and the English on the run
Now, Archbishops they were murdered
(in cathedrals too, no less) -
on the eastern coast, an earthquake
did make Lincolnshire a mess
So why do current English
 moan that modern life is stress?

Now Thirteenth Century England
saw a tyrant brand of King -
John would raise the highest taxes ever,
(worth remembering)
all to fund a pointless battle
(which was lost) on foreign lands,
then on coming home, he caused a civil war
through his demands
Why can't the current Englishman
be happy where he stands?

In Fourteenth Century England
we saw many people die
There were famines when the crops failed,
when the harvest went awry
Wicked Poll-tax, so the peasants
went in mobs to kill the King,
dirty rats were spreading Black Death -
we dug pits for burying
So why do modern Englishmen
complain at everything?

Now Fifteenth Century England,
oh ye time of little cheers
when the battle for the English throne
brought wars for thirty years
now our MP's would arrive at work
well armed, with bat and sticks
all while passing laws that made it legal
burning heretics
Now why do English of today
say England's in a fix?

Now Sixteenth Century England,
oh alas, a time of woe -
new religions forced upon us,
when the Catholics had to go
When a "sweating sickness" struck the land
the towns were much afflicted
Men were forced to take up archery,
much peasant lands restricted -
and "Bloody" Mary's savage reign,
(much worse than was predicted)

"The good old Days"   Friday May 1st 2009

*"Finding joy in present days a total mystery?
Then make yourself feel better, take a look at history"*.........

When William conquered England
(bringing half his Normans too)
we had a "*Bastard*" French asylum-seeker
as our King anew
We lost all of our traditions
and we had to speak in French,
had our castles taken from us -
oh, it did cause such a stench
Now why do current Englishmen
think life is such a wrench?

The Twelfth Century in England -
oh, ye time of little fun
with the Scottish through the borders
and the English on the run
Now, Archbishops they were murdered
(in cathedrals too, no less) -
on the eastern coast, an earthquake
did make Lincolnshire a mess
So why do current English
moan that modern life is stress?

Now Thirteenth Century England
saw a tyrant brand of King -
John would raise the highest taxes ever,
(worth remembering)
all to fund a pointless battle
(which was lost) on foreign lands,
then on coming home, he caused a civil war
through his demands
Why can't the current Englishman
be happy where he stands?

In Fourteenth Century England
we saw many people die
There were famines when the crops failed,
when the harvest went awry
Wicked Poll-tax, so the peasants
went in mobs to kill the King,
dirty rats were spreading Black Death -
we dug pits for burying
So why do modern Englishmen
complain at everything?

Now Fifteenth Century England,
oh ye time of little cheers
when the battle for the English throne
brought wars for thirty years
now our MP's would arrive at work
well armed, with bat and sticks
all while passing laws that made it legal
burning heretics
Now why do English of today
say England's in a fix?

Now Sixteenth Century England,
oh alas, a time of woe -
new religions forced upon us,
when the Catholics had to go
When a "sweating sickness" struck the land
the towns were much afflicted
Men were forced to take up archery,
much peasant lands restricted -
and "Bloody" Mary's savage reign,
(much worse than was predicted)

How would some current English cope
in old times, thus depicted?

Seventeenth Century England -
Pleasant times? Well, not a lot!
They tried to blow up Parliament
in dark November plot
Plus Civil wars, that lasted for
a good five bloody years
Then Cromwell outlawed all our fun -
including Christmas cheers,
and Plague returned - "Bring out your dead"
was ringing in our ears
So why do current English
think they live in wretched years?

Now Eighteenth Century England
saw harsh times that did embroil
the Industrial Revolution
and decades of slog and toil
Great factories, and steam, and smoke, and soot -
and child labour
when iron balls of poverty
chained every man and neighbour
(Add to that, we had non-English speakers
on the throne!)
So why do modern English have
this pessimistic tone?

Now Nineteenth Century England -
near the worst that time records,
when the workers lived as lepers
and the rich folk lived as lords
There was slavery in abundance,
prisoners shipped to Oz by boat
whilst a huge percent of English
did not even have the vote
To English moaners of today -
review, and take a note!

Twentieth Century England
sweated trouble from her pores
when (at least) ten of the hundred years
were spent on fighting wars

We've seen massive unemployment queues,
"real" poverty that grew,
not forgetting all that rationing
when ended, World War Two
We just coped with what life threw at us,
it mattered not a jot -
Why is it people round today
aren't happy with their lot?

Now please compare that list of woe
to England's modern age,
when in this time of comfiness
we've reached the very stage
where everybody has TV
and most have mobile phones,
now many have the Internet -
still everybody moans!
Yet modern life does spoil us so
okay, it's not a breeze -
but recognise, we can do pretty much
just as we please

Now "Black Death" does not trouble us -
"The Plague", no need to fear
and earthquakes seem unlikely too
no famine, will come here
no tyrant Kings to bleed us dry
and drag the country down
no bloody civil wars will rage
twixt' Parliament and Crown
So please shut up all Englishmen
who dream nostalgic ways
I won't be told that things were great
in good, old-fashioned days ...

"Three cheers for Mr Colston"   Monday May 11th 2009

"A further dig into history —because nostalgia ain't what it used to be"..............

Three cheers for Mr Colston!
and halls named after he
Whose profits (and the Empire)
were built on slavery
Gold, he liked to trade in
and ivory was a fave
sugar made his profits sweet -
but none so much as slave!

Hooray for Mr Colston!
The saviour of the poor!
Who also sent poor Africans
on transatlantic tour
That blot upon our landscape -
that episode of shame
that Mr Colston did partake
in our fair city's name

Now sometimes in the Centre -
I'm walking down his street
and often think "what would I say?"
if we should ever meet
I'd say "Hallo there Eddie -
you helped old Bristol out
and did our local schooling proud
by throwing cash about"

"But as for trading people,
oh, you naughty little man -
because of your involvement
I refuse to be your fan
You won't catch me sat in your place,
no concert, gigs - but then!
Just remembered, I went there
to hear one Tony Benn"............

Colston's School, Bristol

"Our Noble Family" (or, 'An Address to Queen Bess')
Saturday May 16th 2009

"A letter I sent to Her Majesty"............

Queen Bess! Your Holy Royalness!
Oh, if I may humbly address -
the country's in a sorry mess,
I trust, like me, you feel the stress?
But if I may suggest, Queen B,
(I'm 'umble, but it seems to me) -
your family wealth is at the core,
the problem lies within *your* door......

A crown does sit upon your head,
yet you don't need to leave your bed -
the Monarchy is past it's prime,
the Royals are a waste of time
This isn't how it's meant to be -
it's just genetic lottery,
you un-elected Heads of State
are born to rule by twist of fate

They say you work, but I can't see
how cutting ribbons earns a fee,
you fly around the world on tour,
it's not a job - a pleasant chore
The final choice is yours to take
on Acts of law that MP's make -
why should you even have a say?
You're *un-elected*, by the way!

You've got no call for NHS,
get instant treatment, nothing less!
No need to queue with all the rest -
your doctors are the very best!
Will Andy fly to golf today?
His helicopter knows the way!
Does Eddie work a *Nine till Five*?
Or need to slog to stay alive?

Is Harry on the town tonight?
Falling drunk or in a fight?
Will he be in fancy dress?
Turning up as Rudolf Hess?
Now what is Charlie's daily role?
He's stinking rich, yet on the dole -
he stumbles, stutters, in a trance,
says "look at me, I talk to plants!"

Your Philip is not etiquette,
now *every* Nation - he's upset
With "slitty eyes" and "throwing spears",
he's getting worse, despite his years
Asylum seekers are a drain?
Oh who says that? Now use your brain -
cuz' funding Royals, in my view
is public money down the loo

To members of the Royal House -
what makes you want to shoot the grouse?
And members of the Royal Box -
why do you wish to hunt the fox?
I just can't help but think, Queen Bess,
we have ourselves a Royal mess -
while England's in a stack of trouble,
you're safely in your private bubble!

Oh pardon Ma'am, but can't you see?
That you're a *dear* anomaly,
the silver spoon, the golden cup -
a loop-hole that needs closing up!
Now this is why I like to curse
the contents of the Royal purse -
and such a person as I am,
so apt to throw toys from my pram!

Oh Queenie, I have left this out,
(more careless words that I do spout!)
for though you think I've got *'a neck'* -
don't want to see it on the deck!
If you think that I lack reason
you may accuse me of *'High Treason'* -
these words will not be public-said,
for I would like to keep my head!

but -

"Why must we bankroll wastes of space –
I think that it's a crime!
The Royals aren't a special case –
Expensive wastes of time!
Like parasitic leeches,
they are sucking on our blood -
they're good-for-nothing scroungers
and the Windsor's name is mud!

So sell off Royal assets –
and pension off the Queen
Then give to those who need it –
those who haven't got a bean
The Monarchy has had it's day,
so we should let 'em know -
Three hundred years is long enough –
it's time for them to go!"

Oops!!

Alas! Alack! Why did I scoff?
For certain now, my head is off!
And to the 'Tower' I must go -
'twill be a sorry tale of woe!

So for my nasty, crude outburst
my fate's the same as 'Charlie First'!
That tirade's put me in the stew -
all in the name of 'Bessie Two'!

I think I need a little crop -
my head will in a basket, drop!
They'll call me "traitor", "headless swine",
and bury me at four foot nine!
Oh Queenie, did I say at all (?)
that it was nothing personal -
the system is the problem here,
your person, I would never smear!

I only want the best for you -
a cottage with an ocean view?
There has to be another way,
instead of what we've got today!
Too late for me, I'm for the chop -
a little bit, I'll 'have off top'!
Now to the 'Tower', it's too late -
prepare to meet my sorry fate........

"Our Noble Leader" (or, 'An address to Mr Brown')
Sunday May 17th 2009

"A letter sent to Downing Street"..........

"Oh Mr Brown, oh Mr Brown -
why *do* you wear that sorry frown?
You've spent more cash without a moan
than any Scot I've ever known!
And Mr Brown - oh, Mr Brown -
how well you wear the UK crown,
you got yourself the job you craved
(a shame the Bankers mis-behaved!)

They've made your job a whole lot worse -
no wonder that you swear and curse
(your predecessor is to blame -
now let me think, oh, whatisname?
the last bloke who was in your chair,
a blighter known as Tony Blair!)
so whisper now, give me a wink,
cuz' I do know what you must think:-

*"I've been stitched up like a kipper
by a toothy little nipper -
who waited till the time was fit,
then went and dropped me in the s--t!
Oh Tony Blair, oh Tony Blair -
you haven't played it fair and square,
you've kept me waiting all these years,
now gone and left me in arrears!"*

Yes Mr Brown, oh *now* you see
that Tony timed it magically -
that clever chap, he always knew
an economic storm would brew
cuz' he had one eye on the clock,
and left you with a 'Northern Rock'!
Thought *"crisis looms, we can't afford -
I think I'll pass it on to Gord!"*

There *is* one thing you could have done
(as you were spending cash for fun) -
why did you hit the brakes too late
when splashing out at speedy rate?
As Chancellor, you spent the loot -
our Services *did* bear the fruit,
but signs were there, you didn't see
cuz' you were on your spending spree!

Now dodgy business was afoot,
the banking thing would go kaput!
Whilst you were busy getting crowned
big bonuses were handed round!
You hadn't thought to fix the roof
(which may have been a little goof!),
and greedy, double-dealing chaps
sent banks into complete collapse!

Along *you* came and said *"Oh dear!
What do I find myself with here?
The market's crashed from deep within,
now finance has gone in the bin!"*
So we did have to bail 'em out -
a travesty, without a doubt,
and things have never been the same -
cuz' guess *who* was charged with the blame?

Our spending power's all dried up,
there's only dregs left in the cup -
your Darling's got an awful job
to play around with a few bob!
It's put you in a sour mood,
you've put on weight, yet off your food -
and 'Tory Boy' looks all anew,
now Davy's running rings round you!

I trust your 'clunking fist' is fit?
(The one that Tony did admit
would strike young Davy quite a blow
on Wednesday's Punch and Judy show!)
The thing that get's me curious,
is why you get so furious -
you smashed a table, broke a chair?
I hope that cat is safe in there!!

But Mr Brown, I do declare
you're looking something of a square -
I think an early night is wise,
you've giant bags under your eyes!
Now how on earth do you suppose
that you'll compete with Tory foes,
you walk as if you're on hot coals -
you're way behind in all the Polls!

And who on earth but *you* can know
how waiting can be very slow -
for fifty years you've wanted *it* -
the job that makes you want to spit!
Now you have found, unhappily,
tis' not all it's cracked up to be -
you've *not* committed massive crimes -
you're just a victim of the times......

The man was *right*, the time was *wrong* -
it's why I write this sorry song -
the fag-end of New Labour's here
and surely now, the end is near
But Mr Brown, oh can't you see (?) -
if you had played it differently,
and pushed your case in '94 -
then shoved young Tony out the door!

It's too late now, oh dear, alas!
And all good things must come to pass -
for though you stagger weary on,
the country wants a 'Tory con'!
I guess we're now a year away,
but under Blair, I'd have to say -
elections *would* be won for fun,
oh Mr Brown, what *can* be done?"

The 'New Labour' Project, 1997 – 2010.......gone, but not forgotten.......

R.I.P.

"The Celebrity Chef" Friday May 22nd 2009

"I've been watching those cookery programmes again".........

If reluctant to hear bitchin'
when you walk into your kitchen
don't invite a Scottish sinner
in your home, to cook your dinner

Lingo of the crudest level
naughty words straight from the devil -
this is what you're apt to hear
if you should find that Scotsman near

It's not merely quiet mutter -
full-blown language from the gutter,
whispered not in gentle tones
but bellowed-out expletive moans

So if you cannot stuff a chicken
and you're prone to finger-lickin',
please avoid his place of work
Or you'll be called a f---ing jerk!

26/5/1999 (two minutes of torture) Tuesday May 26th 2009

"In which the Red Devils unleashed the forces of hell.........."

It's live from Barcelona - two minutes say the clock
Bayern one, United nil - United on the block
Manchester are pressing, the Germans looking firm -
Surely they can't win from here - yet in my seat, I squirm......

United win a corner, so Beckham takes the ball
and from the left he floats it, now it drops amongst them all
There is a little scramble, and the ball falls to a Red
point blank, he tries a right foot shot - eyes closed, I'm filled with dread....

In a flash, the world stands still - the ball moves like a jet -
daisy-cutter, skims the turf.....and crashes in the net!
"Sher-ing-ham" "Sher-ing-ham" screams the TV man
There is a red eruption - they've pulled it out the can!

Disbelief - I shake my head and watch them celebrate
How come they ALWAYS do it - and score so bloody late?
It IS a nightmare, but at least we've still got extra time -
there's eighteen hundred seconds left to overturn this crime

Action replays show the goal, time and time again -
from every angle, fast and slow, to hammer home the pain
So much so, the kick-off's missed - still talking of the goal -
Before we know what's happening, United's on a roll......

They've got ANOTHER corner - it's Beckham's ball once more
He takes it, Sheri nods it on - to Solskjaer - space galore.....
Just a touch, flicks out a leg, the net gapes - three yards out -
ball flies up into the air - oh god! It's IN - no doubt!

It hits the roof, it's in the net and bedlam then ensues -
cuz Bayern were just one-nil up, and now they're gonna lose!
No-one can believe it - the game comes to an end
Bayern one, United two - just cannot comprehend!

Their substitutions changed the game, it played a major role -
with Sheri on for Blomqvist, and Solskjaer on for Cole
A decade on, but THOSE two goals - the story's still retold -
cuz in my dreams at night I see the nightmare still unfold......

"The world's a giant car-park"   Sunday May 31st 2009

"Now here we are, sat in a car – why is it we ain't goin' far?"..............

The world's a giant car-park
(I do travel by balloon)
Now will they say "stop making cars"
when parking's on the moon?

Yet stopping manufacture
will put many in a hole
so are bicycles the answer
with car-makers on the dole?

The world's a traffic gridlock,
one last thing, then I'll depart:-
we'll have to start again, quite soon -
go back to horse and cart

"Twentieth Century Britain" - Part One
Thursday June 4th 2009

"A message for Public speakers. This Poem is NOT - under any circumstances - to be attempted by the out-of-breath. You have been warned! 1900 – 1920

Here it is, our history
in form of verse and rhyme
it's one hundred years of Britain,
or a century of our time

In 1900, British troops
were slaughtered on a hill
though this battle was at Spion Kop
the war continued still.......

In 19/1, Victoria -
God rest her mighty soul
twas a giant of an English Queen -
the longest in that role

In 19/2, a new king, enter-
Edward, crowned at last
True, the old Queen long had feared this day
but now her time had passed

03 saw the strangest weather strike
that England's known -
As Saharan dust had tainted rainfall
with a bloodied tone

In 04, Russians got things wrong
at sea, near Dogger Bank
'cause when firing at the "enemy"
mere fishing trawlers sank.....

In 05, "Launch the Dreadnought" -
it's the prime of battleships
"Britain wants the greatest Navy -
We've got Germans to eclipse!"

In 06, Liberal landslide!
Balfour's Tories booted out -
appetite for social reforms
had resulted in a rout

07 came the "Mud March",
which had started in Hyde Park
A campaign of "Votes for women NOW!"
and all that Suffrage lark

In 08, an Italian is disqualified -
a pity,
The Olympic marathon is held
at London's old White City

In 09, "People's Budget",
"Now let's Super-Tax the rich
and please vote for Old Age Pensions" -
was the general Liberal pitch

1910 saw something strange
so high up in the sky -
as the tail of Halley's Comet
could be seen by naked eye

11 saw a new King
who was crowned George number five -
but his suspect cousins from abroad
meant war would soon arrive.......

In 1912, Titanic sailed -
but plunged in oceans black,
Meanwhile, Captain Scott went to the Pole -
alas, he'd not come back.........

It was 13, at The Derby
when the King's horse came to pause -
'cause thrown in it's path, a suffragette
was martyred for the cause

In 14, came a single shot
that changed world history -
it would kill Archduke Franz Ferdinand,
......four years catastrophe...........

15, mud and rats and lice,
barbed wire and poisoned gas
and then, invasion at Gallipoli
brought slaughter, death - en masse.....

16 saw the Somme Campaign
alleged, would turn the tide
but, four hundred thousand killed
it was, pure bloody suicide

In 17, war rumbled on -
a nightmare stuck in mud
it was a never-ending stalemate,
was a Europe soaked in blood

In 18 came the Armistice,
at last the guns fell silent
but never known to man had been
a conflict quite so violent......

In 19, League of Nations
plus the Treaty of Versailles -
sadly, peace was flawed, it wouldn't last -
two decades soon flew by.......

Year 20 saw the Unknown Soldier
honoured in November
and then every year, eleventh day
with pride, said "We'll remember"............

TO BE CONTINUED...........

"The man in the stove-pipe hat" Saturday June 13th 2009

"Brunel.......the man.......the bridge.......the hat.......the cigars.......the legend"...........

There was a man called Isambard,
who smoked big fat cigars
..It said upon his business card -
......"I'll build a bridge, it isn't hard -
..........the thing will span two hundred yard -
up high, next to the stars!"

"Engineering revelation!"
boasted he on his CV -
.."I've had a sterling education -
......when in London, built a station -
..........high-tech railways for the Nation!"
(such a show-off, he could be)

"I've learned the trade from my old man,
(that's Marc Brunel to you) -
..now within our little clan -
......we built a tunnel, and it ran -
..........under the Thames, a masterplan!
(and they thanked us for it, too!")

This genius, I understand
was Master of his line -
..he cut his railways through the land -
......his fancy tunnels, ready-planned -
..........his pretty bridges, in demand -
(these were all in his design)

His atmospheric railway line
was laid near Devon sands,
..The Teignmouth/Dawlish stretch is fine -
......a journey no-one could decline -
..........of Brunel, yet another sign -
that he mastered English lands!

The railway tracks, he re-designed,
new rules he had applied
..the narrow gauge, he re-defined -
......invented "Wide", then changed his mind -
..........new "Narrow" was then re-assigned -
then saw him satisfied!

"Great Western" was a ship he made
(now what a grand old name!)
.."Great Britain" next, which made the grade -
......"The Eastern", in the next decade -
..........all three put rivals in the shade -
Brunel took full acclaim!

He practiced his "Suspension" theme
on London's River Thames,
..so he did form a little team -
......which built a cockney-walkers dream -
..........it made the London people beam -
(twas another of his gems!)

He started on his Bristol type
in Eighteen thirty-six,
..But there had been a lot of hype -
......with progress slow, they said "it's tripe!" -
..........so Brunel frowned, chewed on his pipe -
and said - "I'm in fix!"

Two pretty towers, made of brick
with mammoth rods of steel,
..of all his things, this was the pick -
......yes, this was Brunel's greatest trick -
..........but now he started feeling sick -
coz' his workload was unreal!

Alas, he wouldn't see it done
(his bridge next to the stars),
..his lifestyle wasn't full of fun -
......his working days would over-run -
..........now Doctor's orders, he would shun -
and STILL smoked fat cigars!

It opened up in Sixty-Four
the Public said – "At last!"
..eighty yards up off the floor -
......a monument that we'd adore
..........it would be cherished evermore -
Brunel was five years passed !

There was a man called Isambard,
who smoked big fat cigars
..an engineer, who worked so hard
......whose reputation's never scarred
..........who Bristol holds in fond regard -
now high above the stars.......

"Paradise Glossed" - (or, 'Bush and Blair; the Glory Years')
Sunday June 21st 2009

"An internationally-known tale of death and romance"............

(Remember remember,
eleven September -
terror, Osama and plot......

lest we ever forget
that the day of the jet
did murder an innocent lot.........)

(enter George)..................

.....................who after 9/11 made
the strange assumption, much relayed -
the evil-doer was Iraq,
where bad Saddam should face the sack

Bush said an "Axis" did exist,
an evil one, "we must resist",
Iraq was central in his eyes,
Saddam, the devil in disguise

"That vile, wretched, evil pig -
Who does he think, he's "Mr Big"?
That country needs a lesson taught
(a bonus if Osama's caught)"

Thought Bush "I need a partner - if
I go alone, there'll be a whiff,
who can I bring to my crusade
to justify my moral raid?"

"I need a Junior partner - in
my firm, my views he'll underpin
Someone who speaks more clear than I,
who can convince and spin a lie"

He looked across the pond, seeking
a British Junior underling
and there did find, caught in his stare
a British man called Tony Blair

Thus born a partner for his fight,
some said it was love at first sight
so Tony, keen to get on board
went to the States to meet his Lord

Our Tony had a keen desire
to set Saddam Hussein on fire
or maybe, shoot him in the head
or bomb him as he lay in bed

Now Mr Bush did share these views
so he thought they had better choose
on how to justify this aim,
without the people crying "Shame!!"

He thought it wouldn't be an error
to call this act a "War on Terror"
and he now had Blair in his team,
in whom to share this brainy scheme

He said to Tone (in Public Hall)
"I thank you friend, thankyou for all.........
so now, we are joined at the hip
together, we've an iron grip"

"We have no greater friend than you,
your country's backed us through and through,
now shoulder/shoulder we must stand -
together, reach the promised land"

At this, Blair blushed a little trace
aware of cameras on his face
(this mug would now be all the rage -
at last his profile was "World stage"

So he was brought to George's ranch
and there, they sat beneath a branch,
attiring heads with cowboy hat,
they settled down to have a chat

Now straightaway, the knowledge came
their views and thoughts were just the same,
two World Crusaders they would be,
to rid this Earth of anarchy

"If Bin Laden's found, then - great!
but that could mean a little wait
Meantime, here's "Plan of Attack" -
our bandwagon goes to Iraq"

But things weren't simple, just like so
and Blair, he wanted Bush to know
that "U.N. backing must be sought -
before a battle can be fought"

But Tony struggled to contain
the excitement in poor George's brain,
so promised him, he'd do his best
to feather this war-monger's nest

So he went home, to London town
though skipping not, was with a frown
he knew the Public of U.K.
would challenge him and want a say

But Blair would keep his promise sound
to Georgy, now forever bound
he could not bear to see him conned,
and said to Bush:- "My word's my bond"

Blair needed proof Saddam Hussein
was storing nasty things again
in short, weapons of mass distress
we'd told him he should not possess

United Nations did see fit
to send inspectors into it,
and snoop around inside Iraq
to see what's in this weapons stack

The Chief Inspector was Hans Blix
but Blair did go to MI6 -
or was it MI5 (?) - forget,
but either way, his mind was set......

Result of this (in time), was thus -
(it put the fear of God in us),
a document that made it clear -
Iraqi threat was much to fear

Not just his neighbours could he slay,
his rockets travelled quite a way -
in less than minutes, forty-five,
Saddam could blow us all alive!

This WAS a startling revelation -
shockwaves felt, throughout the Nation
but Tony knew he had a case
for slapping Saddam in the face

Yet meanwhile, Mr Blix said "No!
There are no weapons here on show -
unless they're hidden far away,
Saddam is clear of all you say"

But Tony Blair, he would persist -
said "Look, these weapons DO exist!
You'd better tell your boys to leave -
I've got invasion up my sleeve"

Now Blix was not incompetent
but he knew war was imminent
so hurriedly, he'd leave that place -
of weaponry, he'd found no trace

Now Britain's a democracy
and not a grim autocracy
so Parliament would get to vote
on dossiers that had been wrote

By "dossiers", I'll say again
(in case I didn't make it plain) -
"in less than minutes, forty-five -
Saddam could blow us all alive"

Now voting slips were counted out,
result of which, there was no doubt
and what this Poll had brought to light
was Parliament had chose to fight

So just one thing now to address -
the calming of Public distress
the ones who were against the war,
would bring their protests to the fore

Was Feb 15th, two thousand-three
when on the London streets we'd see
a million people, maybe more
protest against immoral war

The "No" campaign was in top gear
the message spoke was crystal clear:-
"Now listen Blair, we know your game -
War in Iraq (?) - not in our name!"

But Tony, he would stand his ground
the wheels of war were going round,
the thing had gathered too much pace
so, "too late now, we're in the race"..........

So Georgy Bush was full of fizz -
his poodle boy had done the biz,
no U.N. backing for the cause,
still, Tony said it broke no laws

Besides, (like George) Tone got the "nod"
a blessing sent, direct from God
(This shows how much had not been learned,
since Cromwell's time had been adjourned)

The upshot of it all was thus:-
invasion ON - despite much fuss
and Saddam, he would lose control
and end up hiding in a hole

His "weapons", they were never found -
Blair's document had proved unsound
Saddam removed, George got his dream,
what price though, for his little scheme?

Of what to do when war was through,
they did not have a bloody clue
and chaos reigned for quite some time,
an anarchistic Pantomime

But in a while, George got his hit,
they found a monster in a pit,
a bearded man, by name Saddam
who came as meekly as a lamb

Now Bush took this bewildered pup
and showed it off, just like a cup
to prove he was not round the bend
war HAD been worth it, in the end

They questioned him (Saddam, I mean)
of answering, he wasn't keen
so never would that man be loose -
he ended up with head in noose

Oh, Georgy now was full of fun
he'd got his target Number One,
though Bin Laden was in some cave -
at least Saddam was in his grave

But contrast this to Tony Blair,
who made his Public want to swear
they christened him a lying hound,
as no crude missiles had been found

Yet unrepentent still was he,
and Georgy too, though more in glee
said Bush he'd sleep safer at night
cos Saddam went without a fight

Now six years on, but in that place,
illegal arms, they'd never trace
yet Bin Laden does still roam free,
and still has nerve to court TV

While Saddam died, with head in noose
the masterminds, they still run loose,
so is the world a safer place
then when Bush/Blair set out their case?

It's up to you, to have your view
Myself, I think that this is true -
even with Saddam departed,
we are worse off than when we started

So what of those protagonists,
who'd sought to fight these "terrorists"?
Bush was strangely re-selected -
likewise, Blair was re-elected

Then Georgy left in year 08
whilst Tone hung on, but went too late -
the war had deeply scarred his reign,
and troubled him, till half-insane......

They thought in their own private way
an "evil axis" they could slay
I guess at least they sort of tried
after three thousand souls had died

But planning a revenge attack
it's best to choose not just Iraq -
(Play "eeny-meeny-miny-mo -
which tyrant would we like to go?")

(Now "Know your enemy", it's said
when seeking forth to cause bloodshed -
no point in going off to strike
on any person you don't like)

So in a way, they paid a price
for seeking not better advice
something ventured - nothing gained
now reputations ever stained

We'd love to make the world a place
of safety for the human race
al Qaeda seems, is here to stay -
and lives to fight another day..................

"The Asda Trilogy" - Parts 1, 2 and 3   Thursday July 2nd 2009

"You're shopping in a hurry? Bedminster is not the place.........I rest my case"............

Part One - "The ten items till"

In the queue at Asda
Why is it people nose?
And peer into my basket
Just to see what I have chose?

Yes, I have ten items -
You do not need to count
It is no more, no less than that -
I HAVE the right amount

And if I hadn't *ten*, but *twelve* -
suppose you would complain?
Gesture to the check-out girl
and make me queue again

Mind your bloody business
It's no concern for you -
Count your own stuff, cuz your still
Behind me in this queue.

Part Two - "Senior Citizens"

Old people always jump the queue
They just don't give a shit
They think because they're eighty-two
They'll get away with it

"Excuse me madam - I was first -
now what's the thinking here?
I was nearly at the front -
then 'Bingo' - you appear!

What's your hurry? What's the rush?
I bet you cannot say
Cuz I've got work, and you've got NONE -
you've nothing on today!"

But no-one tells these people off
and pensioners are clever
they've had good time to work this out,
they've been around forever.

Part Three - "Chip and Pin"

What's the point in speedy tills
for people in a hurry?
For everyone in front of me,
a rush is not a worry

Cuz' every single customer
when getting to the till -
it's credit card and chip n pin
to pay the bloody bill

There's six of them in front of me
and every one's the same -
two minutes each per customer,
six items to their name

What's the point in credit cards
to buy a loaf of bread?
Plastic shouldn't be allowed
it should be cash instead

So what's the deal with speedy tills
when plastic rules the day?
It would have been much quicker
had I queued the normal way.

25/5/2005 (six minutes of ecstacy)
Wednesday July 8th 2009

"When is a football club NOT a football club? When Man United's PLC, but Liverpool is LFC!"................'

It's Liverpool in Istanbul, at half-time three goals down -
They'll never turn this game around to win the Euro crown
But thirty thousand Scousers sing "You'll never walk alone",
this time, surely all in vain - Milan's in comfort zone

The time in minutes, fifty-four - the score has seen no change -
ball comes over, Gerrard leaps - it's in his heading range.......
It's in the net - they've scored a goal! The Reds are off the mark -
they've maybe got the faintest chance, a tiny little spark

He sprints right back for kick-off with just one thought on his brain
as he gestures to the Koppites with "Sing up, we'll score again!"
The time in minutes, fifty-six - the Reds still down, three-one
but Smicer gets the ball, right foot - sees space and cracks the gun.....

It's through the keeper - in again! They've clawed it back, three-two!
Milan's defence in total shock, they don't know what to do
It's now a different ball-game, this match turned upon it's head -
the Reds, once three-nil down, could now come right back from the dead

The time is sixty minutes, now the Reds attack once more -
and Gerrard gets the ball - he's through! Oh god, he's gonna score!
No! He's floored, he's on the turf! Now where's the referee?
Lips on whistle, points - to spot! It IS a penalty!

There's utter pandemonium, now no-one can believe
the way this game is panning out, the wonders God does weave.......
Xabi Alonso takes the ball, he places on the spot -
then, tension showing on his face, begins his forward trot.......

He strikes the ball, goalkeeper dives - he smothers it - no goal!
But still it's running loose in there, it spins out of control.......
Alonso's first to follow up, a fraction 'fore the rest -
and just before the keeper's there, he slides it in the nest!

He'd kept his head, that wily lad, he never lost control -
and how his team-mates dived on him for his heroic role!
The stadium's full of disbelief and Scousers going mad!
The Reds, just now, had lost the game, now they've a launching pad

That's three-all, sixty minutes, when three down, at fifty-four -
or, six ecstatic minutes that we'd remember evermore
There were no more goals after that, a few close shaves, it's true -
but ninety minutes came and went, then extra-time passed too

Result of which, it came to be a "shoot-out", from the spot -
five penalties for each brave team, to win that Euro pot
Now Liverpool would win the day, through who they had in goal -
through cheeky, waving, goal-line tricks from a goal-keeping Pole.......

So Jerzy Dudek, come the end, emerged unlikely hero!
Six minutes though, had changed the game when Liverpool had zero!
When half-time came, at three-nil down - it seemed the game was up
But twenty years of waiting spurred the Reds to win the Cup!

"If I was born in 1937" Thursday July 23rd 2009

"A playful wish.........on entertaining a recent thought that maybe I cannot cope with the modern day 21st Century, and was in fact born thirty one years too late?"

Too young to know that war had broke out
too young to be scared, that's without a doubt
yet old enough still to witness V.E.
to take in the dancing, the joy and the glee

To understand freedom and end of the war
were just the two things we'd been fighting for
pulling together, in spite of the blitz
each man for his brother, the hallmark of Brits

They peppered their bombs upon our great city
we never led down, or wallowed in pity
saw light in the tunnel, things never looked bleak
aware this was history, this time was unique

Then what would follow, the start of an age,
a golden era in which to engage
of building new houses, "Employment for all!"
a new Labour Government had answered the call

It was OUT with the old and then IN with the new
and IN with the Red and then OUT with the Blue -
Nationalisation, and free NHS -
a new Welfare State with a DHSS

Then onto the Fifties and music to shock,
like Haley and Presley and "Rock round the clock"
sheer teenage rebellion, that was the next goal,
a brand new invention we called Rock and Roll

By the time of the Beatles, I'd be into my prime
would be twenty-odd years at that magical time
the Sixties were swinging, exciting and new -
The Stones and Bob Dylan, The Kinks and The Who

No-one can say it was "Run-of-the-mill" -
it was acid, and flowers, and freedom - the pill,
Hendrix, and protest, and Vidal Sassoon,
LSD, hippies - and men on the moon.....

End of that period sees my big watershed -
I would put all that orgy and excess to bed,
by that summer of love, 67, I'd attain -
the grand age of thirty - then, time to abstain

So time to get married, have a couple of kids
even in good times, I'd been saving the "quids"
the Sixties were ending, the Beatles would split
the Seventies were harder, but then I'm "past it!"

2002 would be time to retire -
a hard-working life, now no longer for hire
my kids are grown up and they've made their own way -
I've completed my work, so it's now rest and play

So that was the timeline, my lifetime on Earth,
it's why I have chosen that year for my birth
so then I'd go south, and retire to Devon -
feel glad I'd arrived in the year Thirty-seven.....

"The Politician who told the truth"
Saturday August 1st 2009

(A sleazy satire)
"When going to the Polling Booth, make sure you know who's told the truth"
(All characters in this depiction - should be classed as purely fiction)

The modern Politician's breed -
oh, not a noble one indeed
and since the time of history's youth,
there's barely one who's told the truth!

We all remember Clinton's claim,
he'd not committed deeds of shame,
yet after, heard "that woman's" quotes -
she'd taken down MORE than Bill's notes!

Profumo too, lied to the House,
(as he had cheated on his spouse) -
it made him look a silly clown
and brought MacMillans's Tories down

Lord Archer lied and went to jail -
and Mr Aitken went as well,
John Stonehouse claimed that he was dead (!)
- he was found live and well instead

In short, it's hard to trust MP's,
through donkey's years of rotten sleaze,
(much easier to find a tack
that's buried in a large hay-stack!)

However, 'nough of doom and gloom -
this little verse is in it's bloom,
enough of people we have cussed,
it's time to get into the thrust.......

There IS a Politician round these days,
you CAN trust everything he says -
he met a gypsy in Dubai,
who cursed him so he couldn't lie!

His name? We'll call him "Cyril X",
who was the only son of Rex -
(some old bounder in the sticks,
who'd married Lady Norah Wickes)

But this is straying from the plot,
so picking up with Cyril "Dot" -
(though fortune told in foreign booth,
was unaware he'd tell the truth)

Thus over, his "fact-finding" trip,
his "honest curse" had took it's grip
Yet why he would embrace things true
he frankly didn't have a clue

Now while under this "influence",
he had to meet constituents -
who wanted him to pay a call,
addressing them, in their town hall

So off did he in Jaguar
(though careful where he parked that car -
and round the corner he did put,
so people thought he'd come on foot)

Now took his place upon the stage
(and wished his audience in a cage)
still, thought he'd better make a start -
the sooner then, he could depart

"Good morning, my constituents -
I face you with ambivalence,
but that is neither here nor there -
pray, who has got something to share?"

*"My name is Mabel Doris Jacks,
I'm fed up with my Council Tax -
it's esculating all the more,
yet can't see what I'm paying for!"*

"Oh Mrs Jacks - your Council Tax,
(I note by chance, your hearing lacks)
I promise you, I won't be slow
to look into your tale of woe"

"Now who is next? I've much ado -
What issues has our merry crew?
We really need to reach the crunch -
I'm due at "Christies" for my lunch!"

"Ah yes, I see - right there - right there!
The man sat in the broken chair -
no, not you madam - him behind -
your glasses should be re-designed!"

*"I have a cause that I hold dear,
that justifies your being here -
a problem in our neighbourhood
(not all that far from where you're stood)"*

"I recognise that wrinkled face,
it's Mr Thingy, whats-it's-place?
Now pipe up man, do speak, I pray -
I want to hear what you've to say"

*"I have a problem, for my sins,
concerning those re-cycle bins -
I seem to fill them up too quick,
it really gets upon my wick!"*

*"It seems our council's got a cheek,
they take our c--p not once a week -
now can you wonder why I frown?
These stinking bins do get me down!"*

"Your rotten bins are past their prime?
Oh, come on man - don't waste my time!
What silly things do get you vexed!
Now come on people - who is NEXT??!!"

"My name is Michael Simon Dean -
I want to know - where have you been?
You've not been present half the year -
no-one has spotted you round here!"

"Oh Mr Dean, I do declare -
I've had no ruddy time to spare,
my job dictates I have to fly -
I've been fact-finding in Dubai"

"Mrs Goad - Northavon Road
(a rather meek and plain abode)
I have one thing I'd like to say -
concerning politician's pay"

"We local people watch the news,
so now we've come to form the views -
MP's expenses are the rage,
it seems they can extend their wage!"

"Finances? All accounted for -
on office things, it's quite a bore,
it also pays my Internet,
my typist too (I call her 'pet')"

"And is that ALL you're claiming for?
I hear you're raking cash galore -
we fear this money further roams,
there is this thing with 'second homes'"

"The issue you see fit to raise,
to whom - or what - your money pays.......
just remembered, I should note -
I paid a man, sat in a boat!"

"You paid a man sat in a boat?
Pray, did he get to stay afloat?
Why is it that you ramble so -
we haven't got all day you know!"

"Oh yes, a man sat in a boat!
I can confirm - he stayed afloat,
the reason that he got my vote -
'five grand', said he would clear my moat!"

**"So Cyril X - we've heard you quote,
you paid a man, (who got your vote),
to stay afloat, sat in a boat -
and clear your moat - that gets our goat!!"**

"I am sorry to be a pain,
now please allow me to explain -
my second home's a castle *dear* -
not cheap to run, let's make that clear!"

"I roam the peaceful green surrounds -
idyllic, rural country grounds,
now there, my castle proudly stands -
the noble home my job demands!"

"A moat does ring my castle fair -
(this does need tender loving care),
it's purpose, let there be no doubt -
to keep you urban riff-raff out!"

"So now and then, it needs a spot
of clearing out, and all that rot -
a dredging job in all but name,
that is my boatsman's little game"

"The problem is, this thing ain't cheap
and moats, they tend to be quite deep -
still, not to worry - I'm no fool -
the Public's my financial tool"

"Now where was I? I lost my thread -
ah yes, the place I rest my head,
in which I live just like a lord,
(a dwelling YOU could not afford)"

"Alas, alack! Life is so mean!
My swimming pool does need a clean,
my castle wall's displaying cracks -
tis' funded through your Income Tax!"

"My third home does bring in the rents -
it's mortgage is a claimed expense -
I paid it up three years ago,
still, who will ever get to know?"

"I am a connoisseur of wine -
another hobby *dear* of mine,
my vintage classics have endured -
I'll need to get the lot insured!"

"You're paying all my travelling fees,
plus all my foreign spending sprees -
your tips come handy at the "Ritz" -
last year, you sent me to the "BRiTS!"

When trains are late, well - 'life's an ass!'
but 'least I get to go "First Class!
You can't expect a chap like me
to share trips with the likes of 'thee!"

"I've bought an honour for my friend,
upon your loot, it did depend -
the biggest thing that cash affords,
He's now sat in the House of Lords!"

"I'm looking for a new side-line,
now how's THIS for a nice goldmine -
a fast-track UK Passport den
for rich Egyptian businessmen!"

My eldest boy's at Public School,
we wrap him up in cotton-wool,
his fees topped up with Public dough -
well, all these things add up you know!"

"Don't say my snout is in the trough,
I'm just an good, old-fashioned toff -
I'm on the fiddle, to the core -
so 'nudge-nudge, wink-wink - say no more'"

"Don't fear that it's all doom and gloom,
cuz in my heart, there's loads of room -
there's space in there for all of you,
now here is what I'm gonna do - "

"Next time I'm at a big debate
(the 'House of Commons', I relate)
I'll ask the questions for some cash -
show me the colour of your stash!"

"I know somebody will suspect,
but my good name, you will protect -
so with my loot, your MP hopes
you'll stick it in brown envelopes!"

"Nobody to accept my offers?
Have a think and raid your coffers,
meantime people, got to dash -
methinks tonight, I'm on the lash!"

"I'll leave you to your sorry fates -
my mistress patiently awaits!
We're shacked up at the "Ritz" tonight,
as "Mrs X" has missed her flight"

"I need to keep my bimbo sweet -
we've heard the sound of tiny feet,
so help me keep her manner mild -
she's bearing me a love-child!"

"To 'Christies' now, without delay,
you're paying for my lunch today -
my motor's round the corner put,
to thus appear, I came by foot!"

"So 'Tally-ho!' - and all that rot,
away I merrily must trot –
I beg to leave you in the stew,
with this, I bid a fond - adieu!!"

"Twentieth Century Britain" - Part Two
Tuesday August 4th 2009

"The continuation of a Public-speaker's nightmare. Second episode, 1921 – 1939"

In 21, a new "Free State" -
saw Ireland cast away
I mean, at the least the major southern part -
the Ulster bit would stay

22 saw Howard Carter find
exciting things -
such as Tutenkhamun's resting place,
the Valley of the Kings

In 1923 we heard
the sound of Big Ben's chime -
it had been broadcast on the radio
and heard that way first time

In 24, a Labour win!
But it lasted not a year -
they would lose the nation's trust
because of Communistic fear

In 25, John Logie Baird
invents the first TV
which would be followed shortly after
with the start of BBC.....

In 26, a General Strike
called by the T.U.C.
Claimed "Support the Miners" as it's cause -
nine days of mutiny.......

27, the bid to keep
the Cup in England fails
as Cardiff win the blasted, bloomin' thing
and take it back to Wales

In 28, the Suffragette Campaign
achieved it's aim -
it saw ALL British women granted votes,
their rights were now the same

In 29, MacDonald's back
as Labour win the vote
but financial crash across the pond
would virtually sink the boat.....

In 30, "Airship 101"
would crash on maiden flight
but then Amy Johnson flew solo
and got to Oz alright

In 31, financial pain -
the British "Great Depression",
so while Labour went, MacDonald stayed -
in National Coalition

In 32, mass hunger march -
by thousands unemployed,
Cry - "Means-testing jobless benefits -
an outrage to avoid!"

In 33, the sighting of a creature
in Loch Ness
But then was it just a silly hoax,
or nature to address?

Year 34, at Clydebank
saw the launching of "Queen Mary",
whilst for motorists
to pass a driving test was necessary

In 35, the last bow of
King George V would be
the occasion of His Majesty's
great Silver Jubilee

In 36, we had THREE Kings,
saw death and abdication -
so George 6 remained
whilst Edward chose his love over the Nation.......

In 37, the Duke of Windsor
(former King I mean) -
he did visit Hitler in Berlin,
for Brits, an awkward scene

But in 38 came Chamberlain
to take away our fear
("Peace in our time"? - your joking sir,
it's war within a year).......

In 39, we warned him
but then what did Hitler do?
He saw Poland was invaded
hence, the start of World War Two...............

TO BE CONTINUED.......

"Three Cheers for Mr Plimsoll"
Thursday August 6th 2009

"A well-known local pub chant that I heard being sung in great gusto among some of the lads in the 'Barley Mow' last week"......

Three cheers for Mr Plimsoll!
and lines named after he
'twas said he was the sailors friend,
he made them safe at sea
He stuck up for the railways -
he stuck up for the poor -
and then he badgered Tories
who were *stuck-up* all the more!

Hooray for Mr Plimsoll!
He should have won a gong -
the chap who was a Bristol boy,
(but didn't stay too long)
He was friendly with the Miners -
He liked the Liberals too -
became MP for Derby
and the beer he liked to brew!

His nautical invention
was a neat, high-water mark -
twas placed upon the hull of every ship -
not for a lark!
It would stop much overloading,
henceforth making hard to sink -
if you disobeyed it's warning,
you'd be sent unto the clink!

Now when I see his statue
I do say "Hallo there Sam!
Oh, you made the oceans safer-
(others didn't give a damn)!
You're well thought of in Bristol,
they do say 'A chap so fine!'
and sailors sing 'Oh thank god
for the good old Plimsoll Line!'"

"B.I.G. B.A.L.L.s (or, 'The Great Balloon Hunt')"
Sunday August 9th 2009

................*(An Aero-naughty-cal tale)*..............
*"Bristol's In Gridlock! Balloons Are Looming Large! But **who** is watching who?"*

Stave One

Old Alfie Spoons enjoyed balloons
on sunny August afternoons,
so off he went with full intent
of reaching Ashton Court's event

Now Alfie had two kids in tow
son Alfie J and sister Jo,
so off did they in camper van
(would have been quicker had they ran!)

Now leaving home at half past three,
Alfie's intention was to see
the famous Friday evening show
and catch the late-night "Afterglow"

But had he left at half past two,
he may have found a shorter queue -
so leaving as he did, from Bath
found cars a-plenty in his path!

Although the traffic line was slow
it was in fact, the *status quo*
cuz' every Friday was the same -
though, worse still when "Fiesta" came!

At last, reaching the edge of town
the family faces were a-frown -
"Oh god, the nightmare does unfold -
the longest queues in time untold!"

It's fair to say, the kids did fret -
nay, they were getting most upset!
Now, children are hard to amuse,
and in good time, they'll blow a fuse!

*"Now Father, I am Alfie Spoons,
I do intend to see balloons -
but with our current lack of pace
we may as well go back to base!"*

"Oh son of mine, pray, do decline
to fill me in on our deadline -
now can't you see, I do my best
to get us to this *"Aero-Fest"*?

*"Now Father, I'm your daughter fair,
you speak as if without a care -
this waiting does get on my wick,
now can't you see how time does tick?"*

"Oh daughter fair, how very dare!!
Your moaning brings me to despair!
I *am* aware of ticking clocks,
but look ahead, and note the blocks!"

*"Father, I'm your son and heir -
it seems we have no time to spare,
our plan we may have to abort -
we won't make it to Ashton Court!"*

"Oh son and heir, I'd like to share
the info that your brain is bare!
Balloons won't fall into our lap -
take my advice, and shut your trap!"

*"Father, I'm your second-born -
now I advise you - sound your horn!
Unless you give a good, hard blow,
we'll barely make the "Afterglow!"*

"Oh second-born, I hear your scorn
and note the long face you adorn -
I *am* aware of Evening Glows,
but see how bad the traffic flows!"

Along they crawled, with pace of slug,
no zip or whizz, was more a-chug,
with cars ahead, and cars behind -
the traffic jam was most unkind!

Now much amused were those on foot,
who'd left their local cars a-put -
now they began to sally out
and chuck their witty jibes about!

Said one *"Ahoy there, tally-ho!!
- you'll never make the 'Evening Glow' -
we see these queues but every year,
the Ashton roads are never clear!"*

"Then pray, bystander, if you will,
to answer *this* with all your skill -
now can I get to Ashton ridge
by whizzing over Brunel's bridge?"

*"Alas, alack - it's 'No', I fear,
they close that bridge down every year!
Now for the course of the 'Fiesta' -
Brunel's staff are on 'siesta'!"*

"Oh *clucking bell!!*" did Alf disclose -
(at least some words that rhymed with those!)
"We'll never get to Ashton Court
on hearing bad news of this sort!"

Now sister Jo, her mobile rang -
"tis' mother dear, oh how's my gang?
now are you sat and having fun,
and basking in the summer sun?"

"Alas, it has all gone ka-put!
In Ashton Court, we've set no foot,
I thank thee for thy ringing bells -
alack, we are stuck in Hotwells!"

To cut a lengthy story short
the journey, they did not abort -
for five long hours they did sit
and wonder "is it all worth it?"

Three sweaty souls did clamber out
from camper van and thus did spout:-
"Oh goodness me, it's not just late -
the time has gone way past half-eight!"

Now as you've read this little verse,
you may have thought "it can't get worse!"
(I mean this family's rotten time,
and *not* the quality of rhyme!)

So what would now re-compensate
the Spoons' disheartened mental state?
Provided there were things *"aflate"*
it wouldn't matter being late

Yet even this sense of fair play,
fate said, it would be took away -
for, looking round the Spoons' did see
a ruddy mammoth wrecking spree!

Now walking here and there, they found
tarpauline spread across the ground -
great baskets sat in flower beds,
much public frowns and scratching heads!

Not one or two balloons were thus,
but three - or four - or five - now plus!
Now eight! Now nine! And now a score!
Now twenty! Thirty! Forty-four!

Now *all* balloons that they had passed -
they would be flying nowhere fast!
Twas' not the mark of idle berk -
a saboteur had been at work!

The common cry - "My sight misleads!
Who has committed foul deeds?
Oh no! This is a frightful blow -
we'll never see these things a-glow!"

Indeed it was so clear to all,
there'd be no decent festival -
these punctured wrecks would *not* fly high
up in the sunny, August sky

To see so much tarpauline slashed
meant aeronautic dreams were dashed,
some ghastly fiend for sure, had struck -
ballooning fans were out of luck!

But *who* would do such wicked things,
and clip *Fiesta's* sky-bound wings?
The Spoons' were keen to learn the facts
of who had done these wicked acts!

And then! A noise that made then jump!
Came from a little grassy hump,
now sitting there, one withered crone -
who had a face as grey as stone!

"Why if it's not old Alfie Spoons -
oh, know ye how I hate balloons!
So I did scheme an evil plot -
thus early came, and popped the lot!"

The author of this evil rant?
It was the children's wicked Aunt -
(was prone to cook her nasty spells
within her home, down at Hotwells)

Now sported she, a wicked grin
and clearly armed with giant pin!
Which had, it seemed, but caused the sin -
now Alf would take it on the chin!

Cried he - "Oh lord, it's Elsie Spoons!
She's armed with nasty big harpoons!
But why, on sunny afternoons
have you snuck round, and popped balloons?"

"Oh Alfie, I must say my dear,
it is the same but every year -
now in your van, you sit and wait
and queue and rant, because you're late!"

"You never learn that simple trick -
to make good time, cuz' clocks do tick!
In traffic jams, you do get caught -
so you did need a lesson taught!"

"It would have been not half as bad,
but for your rants, that drove me mad!
It was your constant yearly moans
of journeys slowed by traffic cones!"

"Now here you have these kids in tow,
who sit and fret, and "nowhere" go!
So if they MUST enjoy balloons -
then leave by early afternoons!"

"I've barely scratched the surface though,
of why "Fiesta" irks me so -
now here's a little talk I prep,
of trouble on my own doorstep!"

"Three days, a prisoner in my rooms
to get away from traffic fumes!
A whole weekend, locked in my lair
to hide away from this nightmare!"

"No shopping can I do on foot -
like walking throught a load of soot!
It really puts me in a stew,
now even buses can't get through!"

"Don't tell me I should drive my car -
oh, that won't get me very far!
Twould' only push me in the queue
with 'Ashton Court-ers' merry crew!"

"Then coming home, with rest in mind -
when pulling up, what do I find?
Some 'Aeronautical' nut-case
has gone and nicked my parking space!"

"Now can't you see how trippers roam?
I can't but park outside my home!
In Hotwells they do run amok,
the whole weekend, my road's a-block!"

"So every year I'm in the grip
of traffic - how it makes me flip!
Now this is how it hurts my lot -
and yet I ask, it's all - for what?"

"A can of 'Fosters' rising high?
Or 'Sonic Hedgehog' in the sky?
It really makes me blow a fuse!
Such silly things do thus amuse!"

"If punters went up Bemmy Down,
they would still be within the town -
and see all things that skyward roam
until the ruddy cows came home!"

But barely had she ceased her rants
when she was knocked flat on her pants!
A newcomer had joined the fray
and knocked her clean out of the way!

Thus had descended from the skies
a big balloon, to much surprise -
it's basket dropping low, no doubt
had sparked the wicked Aunty out!

As if to rub salt in the wound
it was a *German* who'd ballooned
into the grounds of Ashton Court
and cut old Elsie's speeches short!

So fate had played a trick on she,
the irony was plain to see -
the thing she hated most of all
had struck a blow and made her fall!

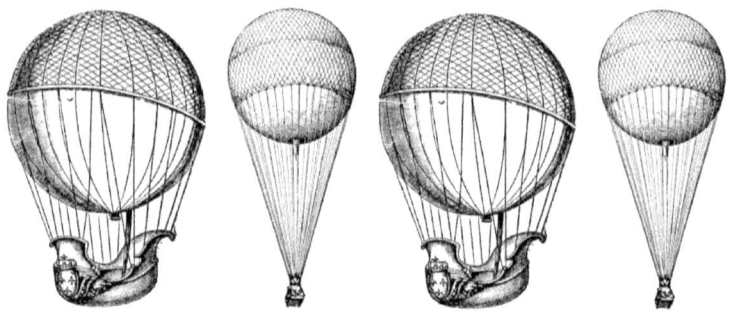

Stave Two

Now this newcomer looked about,
from basket, he did clamber out -
so clearly in a mood for fun,
though checking first, for damage done –

"Panic not! Ze fault's my own!
First Aider for ze withered crone!
She only took a little bump,
but may come out in quite a lump!"

"A-ha! I'm here! A merry trip!
My journey has been quite a zip!
And it does give me much good cheer
to see so many people here!"

Said Alf - "Oh dear, poor show, poor show -
you've struck my sister quite a blow!
But nough' of that, pray do be clear -
what *do* you mean by 'people here'?"

"Can't you see? Do look around -
now all balloons are on the ground!
These foul deeds have taken place -
your *sole* balloon's the saving grace!"

"A fiendish plot's been on the go,
it's dealt 'Fiesta's' fatal blow -
no fancy novelties on show,
no Friday evening 'Afterglow'!"

"Enlighten us, your story share -
methinks you're speaking much hot air!
Pray, tell us in an English style
how you see fit to raise a smile!"

A little crowd had gathered in,
responding to the little din -
now moved to hear with much interest
of foreign tales that had come West

"Herr Schwartzermaier is my name -
I hope you will not thrust the blame,
on me, for fairly crushing down
zis haggard crow, of zis fair town"

"I am surprised by things you say,
balloons and such, not on display -
tis' not ze type of Festival
I've heard that you do host at all!"

"Zis is my first time in your town
(which makes me feel somewhat a clown),
I travel by balloon all year -
had no idea of others here!"

"Your Festival is world-renowned
for viewing people on the ground!
From high, Bristolian occupants
resemble gangs of marching ants!"

"Flying high in August skies,
oh, vot a sight for German eyes -
and such a joy it was, when found
zis half a million, milling round!"

"Your motor cars, tis' very true -
it's quite a merry little queue!
Ze stories that I've heard are right -
from way up there, it's quite a sight!"

"Now I was simply not aware
it was a Festival of Air -
we 'Johnny foreigners' but know
of non-existent traffic flow!"

"Your August Festival's well-known
but for ze way your roads a-groan
beneath the weight of traffic jam
(you Englishmen don't give a damn!)"

"Your gridlock's famed in German lands,
where nobody quite understands
the happy, laid back English, who
so patiently, do sit and queue!"

"Now, Bristol's roads are never bare,
you sit in lines without a care -
it made my countrymen see fit
to send me to take pics of it!"

"So thus, from Munchen I did fly
to see these motors from ze sky -
it IS a shock to see it's all
about balloons, zis festival!"

"I brought my camera here with me
was for my picture-taking spree -
so from my basket I did lean,
tis' such a photogenic scene!"

"And vot a wunder time I've had!
You English must be raving mad -
half a million, travelled far,
for 'Festival of Motor Car'!"

"I do declare, I've seen them all -
the Rover, Renault - and Vauxhall!
Ah! Not forgetting camper van -
nor too, your famous 'white van man'!"

"I'm feeling dry, a little queer -
so for your German guest - a beer!
Ah! See how everybody darts -
my loyal English crowd departs?"

Indeed, the Spoons had heard enough
and had stormed off in quite a huff!
It mattered not, their Aunt was sent
 to get well in the First Aid tent!

So off did they, to camper van,
for they had hatched updated plan -
the rush to leave the Friday 'Fest'
was under way by all the rest!

And so the outward queue began
to trickle out in car and van -
not long arrived, for *no* balloons,
now leaving in five-door saloons!

Now with some luck, the three of them
would be back home by 3 am!
But on one thing, they were all sure -
'Fiesta' trips would be no more!

THE END

"Local news is rubbish"
Monday August 17th 2009

"A well-known pub chant, given an airing in the 'Spotted Cow' last week"............

Local news is rubbish and it don't give me a thrill -
Who wants to know of traffic jams, or garden fetes in Pill?
Local news is rubbish, now I really cannot try
to be amused by Sainsburys, if prices are too high

Local news is rubbish and I really do not need
to know about church jumble sales or roadworks in Broadmead
Local news is rubbish, now I don't want to decide
if Bristol has the need to fund another Park and Ride

Local news is rubbish, see I really cannot take
whether Horfield residents are being kept awake
Local news is rubbish, oh I really do not care
if Bath is losing tourists or if Clevedon's looking bare

Local news is rubbish and I just don't have the time
for villagers in Dundry when their church bell doesn't chime
Local news is rubbish, see I just don't give a damn
to find out whether Gloster Farm is making decent jam

Local news is rubbish, now it really makes me frown
to learn that traffic wardens are all gathering in town
Local news is rubbish and it is no big surprise
to see which Keynsham Bakery has got prize-winning pies

Local news is rubbish - I've no interest in things
like Bath Park has grafitti on it's roundabout and swings
Local news is rubbish - I've seen the BBC -
now I want more National news and switch to ITV.

"I am a child of Thatcher"
Thursday September 3rd 2009

"Local news is rubbish? So was the National news – refer, all dates between May 3rd 1979 and November 22nd 1990. Oh Margaret, dear Margaret – how we miss you".........................

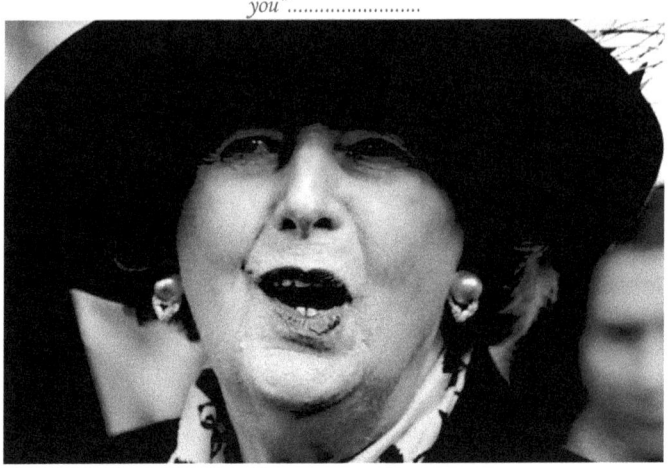

I am a child of Thatcher, it's regrettable but true -
it was as a boy I saw her, twas a dragon dressed in blue
She dreamt economic policies to benefit the few,
then she turned against the miners - waged a Civil War, mark two

She strangled local Government and scrapped the GLC -
thinking "let's consign the working-class into our history!"
"I'll privatise the industries, let's sell the whole lot off!
I want tax cuts for the super-rich – the upper Tory toff!"

I'm one of Thatcher's children - see, there's millions of us too
I just hate the selfish attitudes she tried to hammer through -
Told us "Just be single-minded, quickly grab at what you can -
and don't worry 'bout your neighbour, only you" - her masterplan

"Society? There's no such thing! "It's down to selfish greed -
you see, it's up to individuals to free *themselves* from need"
Three million people on the dole, her friends said "On yer bike" -
"Go look for work, there is no need to riot or to strike"

Her brainchild was the Poll Tax, her unfairest trick of all -
as normal, she would not be swayed - it led to her downfall
Good Queen Margaret, never wrong - "The lady NOT for turning"
yet in Trafalgar Square one day, her effigy was burning

Thought Heseltine – "now here's a whizz, I'll turf the tyrant out!
For far too long, this autocrat's been bossing us about!"
And pretty soon, old Maggie found herself stabbed in the back –
her Tory cronies turned on her from years of taking flack

Then leaving Number 10 at last, we saw her welling up –
Did she think we'd pity her? She'd filled our bitter cup!
...............*I am a child of Thatcher but I never took the bait*
        so I'll lose no sleep when she is dead - in fact I'll celebrate.

"Evolution of the telephone"
Tuesday September 22nd 2009

"In which I applaud the merits of modern technology and advance the opinion that we have thankfully come a long, long way since 1876. Sarcastic? Moi?"..........

When Alexander Graham Bell
invented his device,
maybe benefit of hindsight
would have prompted him - "Think twice"

We've got Apple, Orange, Vodafone
and every kind of brand
bloody ringtones, bluetooth, picture texts -
too much to understand

You get iTunes for your iPhone,
get your Facebook status set -
plus, upload your private movies
and then put them on the Net

Download the latest ringtones,
get free access to the Web,
you can find out what is happening
to your favourite star celeb

We are told to watch "Big Brother"
then "text off" the one you hate -
ditto "X Factor", just use your mobile -
to eliminate

"Text me, Text me - send that song -
and let me see that funny clip" -
"that filthy joke" - "pornography" -
"that smutty little strip"............

Oh Alexander Graham Bell sir,
what have you gone and done?
granted, telegrams were slower,
but then waiting was more fun

I'm all for progress, but I feel like
butting a brick wall -
When all I ever want to do
is make a quick phone call.

(REMEMBER THOSE?)

"The Scotsman's day out in Bristol"
Wednesday September 30th 2009
"A strange tale that was doing the rounds at the "Bag o' Nails" last week".........

A Scotsman fond of drink did come
to Bristol's fair old town
and feeling zoological
thus went to Clifton Down

A teacher of the Maths was he
that man, now he could count!
And loved to climb the mountains high
(that was a high *a-mount*)

He studied all the animals,
then took himself a stroll,
and ended up down Granby Hill
in search of water-hole

Now George (he had been christened)
thus descended to Hotwells
and when in ramble by the docks,
his brain was ringing bells....

Ideas, they rarely passed George by,
so he did think "By George!"
"I'll go and hitch my hiking boots
and hitch-hike to the Gorge!"

Proceeding to his B & B,
he grabbed what he did need -
two boots, and scant amounts of cash,
befit of Scottish breed

He thought - "Before I climb that mount,
a-peckish I will be -
so first, I'll go unto the Pub
and have a spot of tea"

So off did he to "*Merchant's Arms*"
for whisky and a steak,
but George, so normal good at Maths
lost count of his intake

And sampled he, the local brews
six ciders and a sherry -
thus came to be, that adding Scot
did feel a trifle merry!

Now through his Highland lingo
(somewhat slurred) old George was teased -
not worried though, the Landlord
through his takings, he was pleased

But just to make it clear right now,
that he was NOT unkind -
he did have no idea of George's
climbing frame of mind!

Now George saw fit to stagger out,
to end this little orgy -
before someone did spot his gut
and dub him "*Georgy-porgy*"

A climber he had been, that chap
from humble Scots abode
the only hill he'd present find -
just down the Hotwell Road

So swaggered he, with no real grace,
was more of drunken stomp -
now blundered on his weary way
unto his hazy romp

Arriving near the Portway
saw his mind get in a fix -
as his counting wasn't working
and his sight was playing tricks

These things became apparent,
when he looked up to the ridge,
and did see in quite a tipsy way
"double" Suspension Bridge!

Now George, he knew this wasn't right -
his seeing two (or three!),
so continued with this eye-test
viewing the *Observ-atory*

On finding there, again a pair,
thus came to a decision -
he suffered not insanity,
but from the "double-vision"

Yet undeterred did he remain
a climb was in his mind -
no sober drink would pass his lips,
a bed would be declined

So up the Avon Gorge went he
much slipping and a-sliding -
no hat or harness he possessed,
was hardly law-abiding

A ghastly sight, straight up the kilt
with viewed with much dismay
by all and sundry, passers-by
from down the old Portway

Now despite his "said" condition,
by a lucky twist of fate -
the Public, they did see that Scot
ascend at speedy rate

Adrenalin was a-pumping
"Dutch courage" in full flow -
three quarters from the ground was he,
a short distance to go

But flapping over he, did find
a seagull in the air -
then, to his rage discovered
it had pooped into his hair!

Now George, he was a Scotsman,
and a proud one too, at that -
so he raged at this obscenity
(though should have worn a hat)

Now poop in ginger Scottish locks
will make the air turn blue -
his hair had not required a wash,
until this fake *sham-poo!*

Now stood upon a slidy ledge,
of manner, raging bull!
And shook his fist in fury
at offending animal!

A hasty action, which contrived
to make him slip and fall -
and cling upon that slidy ledge
with quite no hope at all!

His fingers, they could not hold on,
his luck, it was amiss -
now all that waited for him was
the fall unto abyss.......

But, what would save that tipsy Scot (?) -
"*Fiesta*" - heaven sent,
as the first weekend in August
meant an annual event -

Page 71

So before he knew his bearings
he was dragged in a balloon,
which continued flying upwards
till it landed on the moon..........

"Twentieth Century Britain" - Part Three
Sunday October 4th 2009

"The next episode of this bizarre epic. 1940 – 1960"..........

In 40, mass withdrawal
but it's glory in defeat
as Dunkirk evacuation showed
we don't know when we're beat

In 41 the bombing raids
continued on our cities,
so it's down the London Underground
for conradeship and ditties

Year 42 saw Beveridge
report on welfare themes,
this would lead to introduction
of full unemployment schemes

In 43, it seemed the speeches
Churchill made were right
'cause we'd rode our luck, survived the Blitz -
got freedom in our sight........

44 saw D-Day,
caught the Germans unaware
and the landings there at Normandy
put victory in our stare

In 45, it's V E Day -
and Churchill's voted out,
as a landslide at the polling booths
sees Labour win a rout

In 46, it's "Nationalize" -
the Bank of England's first
then Gas, Coal, Electric, Water, Steel
would follow in quick burst

In 47, a winter white,
we called it - "The Big Freeze" -
as much heavy snowfall, rationing,
brought England to it's knees

In 48, it's here at last!
"Three cheers for National Health!"
it's free treatment based upon your need
and NOT upon your wealth

Year 49 saw Orwell print a book
of grim prediction
"84" said many, was a call of warning,
not mere fiction

In 1950, British troops
returned to state of war,
their three-year fight to save Korea
and to make it free once more

51 saw Churchill back,
as Tories won the day
by now, the country's tired of Labour
and think Attlee's lost his way

52 saw mourning
as King George would leave the scene,
Princess Elizabeth in Kenya
now returned to us as Queen -

in 53, her Coronation's
broadcast on TV,
plus the famous Matthews' Final match
saw Blackpool win 4-3

It was 54 at Oxford
when the mile was ran fast,
as achieved by Roger Bannister
before four minutes passed

In 55, the "Ladies man"
did enter Number Ten,
it meant that Churchill left for good this time,
now Eden's in the den.....

Year 56 saw British troops
all congregate for war,
however, Eden judged the Suez wrong -
he'd soon be out the door......

In 57, a new PM
was known as "Supermac" -
he said "you've never had things better"
(was this claim a little slack?)

In 58, the dream that died
at Munich, in the snow
so, how good the Busby babes would be
fate said - "you'll never know"......

In 59, new transport,
and it's not so very daft -
in two hours, Dover-Calais -
it's the birth of Hovercraft

In 60, an appointment
that would make rail travellers frown
as Doctor Beeching's job would be to scale
the country railways down.......

TO BE CONTINUED............

"Ode to Autumn" Saturday October 10th 2009

"Now here I sit beneath this tree, so why can't you just leave me be?".........

Oh why do leaves fall out of trees and pile up on the floor?
Tis' slushy mess around my feet, it bugs me to the core!
They're under windscreen wipers and they're blowing in my hair -
they're stuck up my exhaust pipe, oh, they're bloody everywhere!
This season's so depressing, when you know that summer's gone -
so cold, and dull, and wet, then worse - when winter follows on!
I'm finding this downheartning, cuz' I thought I'd write nice things -
alas, it impossible - let's see what winter brings.........

"PC Cobb (Who had a hard job)" Monday October 12th 2009

"The story that was doing the rounds at 'The Grapes' last week"........

PC Cobb was on the beat
when all he wanted was a seat,
"Why can't I have a Panda car -
why do they make me walk so far?"

See PC Cobb, though judgment sound,
was blessed with body fat and round -
God let him have a useful mind
but choice of figure was unkind

Now chasing yobs is pretty tough
when thirty yards, you're out of puff,
so running was a waste of time
when PC Cobb did witness crime

Delinquents, they would laugh at him
and call him names like "PC Slim",
say "no we won't come nice and quiet -
now, Porky pig - go on a diet!"

"They won't let you go in the car,
you push the seat down way too far -
that vehicle won't zip round town,
your travelling puts the tyres down"

Now PC Cobb, he heard these jibes
and thought that it gave out bad vibes -
he worried his unsightly frame
would give the force a silly name

"Now what am I to do?" thought he,
"I let them walk all over me -
I think it's time to change my tack,
or else, prepare to face the sack"

"But how am I to keep my job
when seen by all as "PC Slob?
I cannot dream of staying put,
they know I am not fleet of foot"

Now one fine day came on the scene
a circus, down upon the green
with stalls, and rides, and sundry tents,
and fortunes told for ninety pence

it was a magnet for the yobs,
for idle teens who had no jobs
so to the fairground they did go
in search of trouble at the show

now fortunes told and tents explored,
the yobs did find that they were bored -
though fairground was the plan of action,
"Big Top" was the main attraction

So ambled they, into the tent
the chance of mischief, heaven-sent -
no sooner had they parked their bums,
when came the sudden roll of drums

So in the circus ring there came
some jungle beasts, appearing tame,
no chance that they would harm a soul -
the Ringmaster was in control

But yobs do like to mis-behave,
to play the fool and act the knave,
present a man armed with a whip -
they will decide to give him lip

The lions did receive no cheers
and all the jumbos' heard were jeers,
the fire-eaters got the bird,
for clowns, a round of boos was heard

Now PC Cobb can smell a crime,
that brain of his was in it's prime
and what the yobs had never seen,
was Cobb had waddled to the Green

He'd followed then, that portly gent
and watched them entering the tent,
he knew full well they would be keen
to mischief-make and cause a scene

Now eagle-eyed, this "Plod" did see
a ladder propped against a tree,
thought Cobb "This plan I have makes sense -
it's just the thing for climbing tents!"

So up he went onto the roof,
"no tent too high", here was the proof,
and when at last, he'd reached his goal -
his eye fell on a little hole.....

Now balancing on tarpaulin,
he'd found a rip and did peer in,
the sight that greeted him was thus:-
five yobs were there, creating fuss

And fate had dealt a funny blow -
those idle louts were sat "Front row",
direct below, they could be found
and right beneath his heavy mound

thought Cobb "I've got them in my sight -
my whistle will give them a fright"
But fate had one more trick to play -
alas, the roof was giving way.........

The circus now had one more act
unscheduled though, and that's a fact,
the audience unexpected treat (?) -
dive-bombing cops from sixty feet!

That Cobb fell hard, there's no debate
he crushed that gang beneath his weight,
till all stood up, right out of breath -
six miracles of dodging death

Spectators did let out big cheer,
the loudest that was heard all year,
from idle yobs, came not a peep -
knocked senseless, till lain half-asleep

They'd never trouble Cobb again,
their egos were completely slain
In fact, this gang went seperate ways,
found better things to fill their days

Now Cobb's heroics made the news,
the "Bugle" gave him rave reviews,
yet one decision still faced Cobb -
that's what to do about his job....

the Public, they did want to hear
that bulky copper's new career,
then said the local news announcer -
"Cobb's become a nightclub bouncer!"

thus ends a tale of gallantry,
of roly-poly ex-PC -
once joke of the Community,
now valued stout celebrity...........

"Accents, according to the media............."
Thursday October 15th 2009

"ooooo-arrrrrr, ooooo-arrrrrr, ooooo-arrrrr!!".........

.........Geordie's so agreeable
Scouse indeed's most fashionable
yet Welsh is near intolerable
and Brummie's straight unbearable

Scots, non-understandable
Irish is "boyband-able"
what really wrankles most of all -
Bristolian's unacceptable........

"The Daily Redtop"   Sunday November 1st 2009

"'It was the Redtop wot won it!'(1992) – a rant against nasty news"

Daily Redtops! Scandal rags!
That read like "A B C" -
publications that see fit
for rudeness on Page Three
thirty pages full of sport -
there's news? It's in disguise!
A pull-out section on TV -
the rest is bloody lies!

That Daily Redtop! Scandal Rag!
That brings the country down -
for trashy, low-life, gutter press
this paper wins the crown!
That foul Redtop is to brains
what fags are to the lungs -
if quality's a ladder,
then it's on the bottom rungs

It's jingoistic nonsense -
it's flag-waving gone mad -
it's comic book material
for the clinically sad

That Redtop is to mental health
what sugar is to teeth -
it's purile rubbish on the front -
no better underneath!

If unemployment's going down,
the Redtop's big headline? -
that "so-and-so" from X Factor
has got a speeding fine!
Exam results are much-improved,
what's Redtop's little scoop? -
half-naked "Jungle" has-beens
pictured jumping through a hoop!

More troops into Afghanistan,
what's Redtop got to share? -
the latest football player caught out
having an affair!
More money goes to National Health,
what's Redtop on the front? -
another failed celebrity
in sick "Big Brother" stunt!

But comes Election, then decides
to go all topical -
and does pretend that it's agenda
is political
Then tells us which is right from wrong
and picks it's candidate -
(most often this will be the one
who's chance the Bookies rate)

That scandal-monger! Gossip rag!
That sets tongues wagging so!
That cheap and tacky pile of poo,
I would love it to go!
It's for the hard of learning,
it's a tabloid for the dumb -
but I declare that it's not fit
to even wipe my bum!

A little story of a friend -
the memory's very clear
political allegiances,
she did hold very dear

Now when a mutual friend of ours
rang on her bell one year,
she snapped - although YOU can come in -
DON'T bring that "rag" in here!

That Daily Redtop! Scandal Rag!
It really gets my goat -
you need a magnifying glass
to find a truthful quote!
Why bother cutting trees down
when they should have used as wood?
(And add to that, I've heard the crossword
isn't very good!)

That nasty Redtop! Scandal rag!
Let's bring the "Daily" down!
Or boycott it, ignore
in every city, every town
We're better off without it,
now here's a little caper -
don't let 'em have your cash no more
and buy another paper!

"The Spirit of Women's Rights"
Thursday November 12th 2009

"A short poem about Pankhursts. Their cause. Where did it all go wrong?"........

When fast asleep in bed last week
a dream did chance to be -
in which, if I remember right -
a spirit came to me

Now as I looked, I recognised
(a face, I don't forget)
it bore the very features
of a famous suffragette

It spoke - *"Behold! I bid you well,
one thing (I can't be long) -
The 'Movement' - does it prosper so?
Is womankind still strong?"*

"Oh Christabel, Oh Christabel -
your cause is not advancing -
the only thing they vote on now
concerns "*Strictly Come Dancing*"

And she replied "*No, surely not -
how do you thus derive?
The ladies were so principled
when I was still alive*"

"Oh Christabel, Oh Christabel -
your maidens you do flatter -
their votes go to "*The X Factor*",
but no Election matter"

Said she - *"Not true, it cannot be -
your theory does have failings,
now in my time, for right to vote,
we'd chain ourselves to railings!"*

"Oh Christabel, Oh Christabel -
you're stubborn, like your mother -
the ladies, they *DID* vote last week -
for who would leave "*Big Brother*"

*"Alas, alack - oh woe is me!
I hoped you were mistaken -
but now it comes so clear to me
my cause is but forsaken"*............

.........and with that, she was gone!

"Deals on meals" Saturday November 28th 2009

"A ready-made poem 'to go' – for people in a hurry"........

Now when they said "*square* meals a day", they made you laughing stocks -
they never meant a "meal deal" like a burger in a box!
On such filthy rubbish you see fit to daily dine -
this cardboard cube holds grease and muck "for just £4.99"!

So much for healthy eating, oh how standards do decrease!
No wonder that we're always told the country's gone obese!
"Would you like a drink with that?" - oh god, it makes me sick!
And "won't you have a nice day" - they do think we're bloody thick!

Now whilst these people count their coins, accumulating wealth -
then who gets left to count the cost of daily falling health?
So if you want to throw away your wages on the rich -
then carry on, and chuck your healthy diet in a ditch!

"Loud ugly chap"   **Friday December 4th 2009**

"He who must remain anonymous".........

He's a loud ugly chap -
who never shuts his trap,
who never takes a nap,
who's forever spouting crap

Please someone, take him away,
if only for a single day
Five pounds, to someone I will pay -
to keep the ugly one at bay.

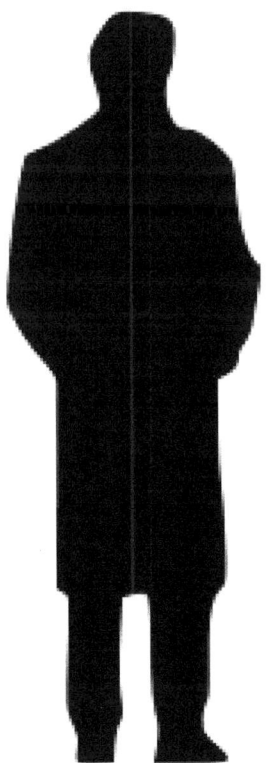

"Paper Man"   Tuesday December 8th 2009

"The story that was doing the rounds at the 'Seven Stars' last week".........

Sitting in the station
is a man of foreign nation
whose usual little caper
is to always read his paper

Buses come and buses go,
people bustling to and fro -
if this man has travelling needs,
why is it then, he sits and reads?

There is no room to sit and wait
for this old man is obstinate -
for him, a wait is not a drag,
but must he read that filthy rag?

Tramps go by and ask for money,
don't they ever find it funny? -
He won't pay them too much attention,
his paper is too good to mention

Midnight's here, it's very black
so business now is very slack,
for one old man, it's still not late -
he's not yet read page forty-eight

Does he mean to stay all night?
Will he leave when it gets light?
His glasses mist, all steam and vapour -
still he reads that bloody paper!

Morning comes and lying dead
is one old man who'd read and read -
he really would have had a ball
to read about his own downfall

The moral of the story is
to widen your activities,
for too much reading, as we see
will end in black eternity........

"The Zzzzz Factor" Sunday December 13th 2009

"Now hit that note, or miss the boat – it's really very clear! And you at home, pick up the phone – or else they're outta here!"........

Come join this queue if you can sing -
we're lookin for the next "Big thing"
If you can win, we'll make you rich
so all we ask is "sing in pitch!"

Walk in this room, let's hear your voice
we'll sit and judge and make our choice,
you get our votes - you're in Round Two -
out of key - you won't go through

Come closer madam, let us hear
I want to listen nice and clear
But as your looks give us a fright
you'll have to sing like Gladys Knight!

Come in young sir, do not be shy,
just stand right there and have a try
Good lord, you've got a big waist-line -
now sing it well, or we'll decline

Who claimed that you could sing my dear?
They're clearly wrong, they couldn't hear!
Either that or they told lies -
your voice will *never* win a prize!

You are the worst I've ever seen -
to call you "dire" would NOT be mean
Who said that you could sing a song?
Oh trust me love, they're very wrong!

You are the BEST we've seen today -
you're in Round Two without delay
I'm pleased to say, it's "Yes" times three -
you're through to Boot Camp, if you're free

"Too young, too old, too fat, too thin" -
your voice is an annoying din
Your future's NOT in showbiz, dear -
and singing's not your next career!

A boy says "Please - Just one more chance?
It's not just voice - I also dance,
and singing's all I ever like -
it will sound better through a mike"

"Listen son, you're leaving here -
I don't know how to make that clear.
Your voice is just not up to scratch -
heard better at a football match"

What a way to spend ten days,
to sit and hear these waifs and strays
We're all relieved when it's the end -
at Boot Camp, riff - raff WON'T attend!

So on they go, you hold the key -
they're whittled down on live TV
then who goes next, it's down to YOU -
"So text us now to put 'em through!"

Ring this number, vote online
and see if your choice matches mine
Text us now, the charge ain't high,
cuz' standard network costs apply

So one by one, they're voted out,
a month of fame, then back to nowt
Not quite up to singing live,
now sadly back to 'Nine till Five'

Then at last, it's down to two -
so "Who wins now, it's up to you" -
the Nation gasps and holds it's breath,
cuz now it's down to sudden death

Here it is world, this is IT -
Now who could sing that extra bit?
Lines are closed now - calls galore!
And this is who you voted for........

Congratulations, take a bow -
he's gonna be a star - for now
The next four weeks are full of fun -
he'll sing the Christmas Number One

You'll hear the song sung by your Winner
whilst you eat your Xmas dinner
With luck, we hope he DIDN'T hear -
his fame won't last into the year

The showbiz world is full of sorrow,
here today and gone tomorrow
"Forgot to say, you'll have ONE hit -
then sorry son, afraid - that's it".

"Early morning" Tuesday December 29th 2009

"Victoria Park, Bedminster, Bristol"

Every morn' I walk the park
and I love to take it in
For just five minutes, there is no sound -
no traffic makes a din

And in the morning sunshine,
the only sound I hear:
My footsteps padding in the frost,
no other soul is near.

"The Tenth Doctor Who"   Friday January 1st 2010

"Troubles in the TARDIS?"

Bring back David Tennant
such a shame he had to go,
even better-looking than myself
(though, not my style to crow)

With big brown eyes and spiky hair,
the ladies hearts he'd win
and he even fought the Daleks
with that cheeky little grin

No wonder Billie Piper
couldn't stand to be too far
even Captain Jack,
he kept the Doctor's right hand in a jar!

Yes, bring back David Tennant
cuz the new one is too young -
I've a feeling 'bout this next guy
that his praises won't be sung

Now reverse regeneration
and bring Davy back anew,
cuz persisting with this "Matt"
will put the programme in a stew

So come on, Mr Tennant
just return to your endeavour -
cuz every Poll does say that you're
the greatest Time Lord ever

But wait, what am I saying -
you fear you'll be type-cast?
and scared that as the Doctor
of this role will be your last?

Then when you carry on your way,
remember as you do -
that along with Thomas Baker,
you're the greatest "Doctor Who"

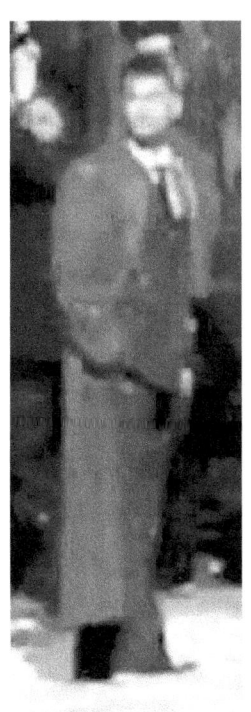

"Doctor Blinker"   Saturday January 2nd 2010

"The story that was doing the rounds at the 'Adam and Eve' last week. (Told here in 'Present tense')"...........

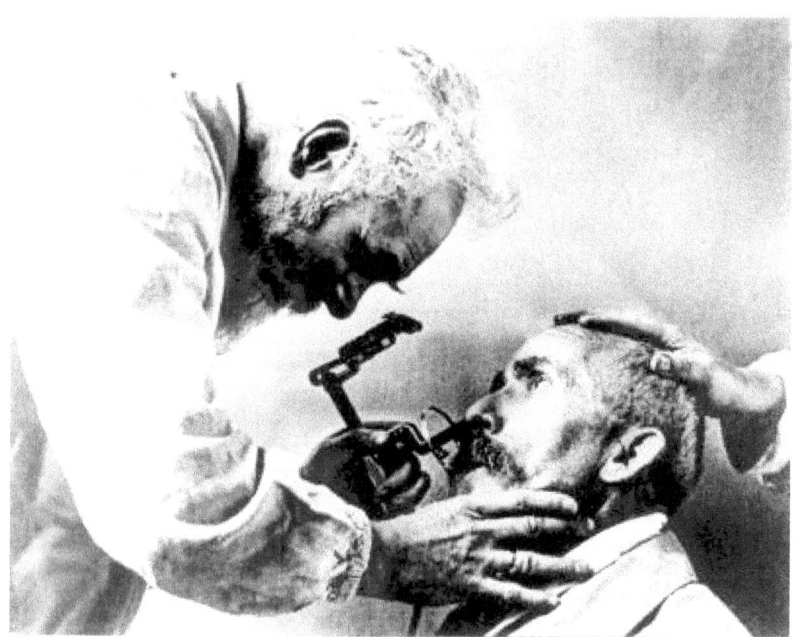

Doctor Blinker's on his way
to treat the patients on display -
but will he have the time to make
an hour for his dinner break?

Broken bones and bellyaches,
nervous people with the shakes -
are examples of the cases
Doctor Blinker this day faces

A chap comes in who says "I'm sick",
so Blinker says "I've just the trick -
now take these pills but twice a day
and slurp this juice without delay!"

Doctor Blinker slams a door
when a woman brings a labrador
"Oh madam, take away your pet -
you really need to see a vet!"

A congregation won't rejoice,
for Father Jack has lost his voice -
but Doctor Blinker says "Drink this -
and give your Sabbath date a miss"

"I really cannot kip at night" -
says Farmer Bill, (who looked a sight)
"Then have you tried to count your sheep?
That usually send 'em off to sleep!"

Doctor Blinker had a hunch
he would not have the time for lunch -
he *would* have had a bite to eat,
but for the tramp with blistered feet

Bob the butcher could not gloat,
because of soreness to his throat -
says Blinker "I will stop your pain,
you'll soon be chopping meat again"

Then Blinker tends an achy lobe,
he tells the girl "let's take a probe -
Oh this is why your hearing lacks,
your blasted ear is full of wax!"

A sailor says "I've taken ill,
I cannot sail without a pill -
Doctor, let me miss the boat,
by writing me a long sick note?"

"Sailor, sailor, can't you see?
I've got a busy surgery,
I'll only offer you a tip -
Get out, and go onboard your ship!"

Blinker is at his wits end -
his patients drive him round the bend
"When will I get to leave?" he thinks,
"I am in need of forty winks"

Doctor Blinker's had enough,
his workload has been pretty tough
"I really am not well" says he -
I need to see my own G P"

So Blinker thinks "I want to quit -
my patients make me want to spit!
Now in this job, I cannot cope,
I'll soon hang up my stethoscope"

"But wait a minute, let me see -
there's nothing else I want to be,
as unemployment brings low pay -
I think I'll quit another day!"

"Twentieth Century Britain" - Part Four
Monday January 4th 2010

"Next instalment – 1961-1979"

In 61, Polaris submarines
at Holy Loch!
They were Yankee missile-launching things
that Scots had tried to block

In 62, "Night of Long Knives"
(a scheme of "Supermac"),
when a Cabinet re-shuffle
meant a load would get the sack

In 63, four moptops
got their debut number one,
it was the start of Beatlemania,
the decade of much fun

64 saw "thirteen years
of Tory mis-rule" end
as Wilson's Labour Party won at last -
on Harold, we'd depend.....

In 65, at London's Docks
the cranes dipped in salute
as down the Thames sailed Churchill's coffin,
twas a fitting State tribute.....

In 66, we won the war,
at least - it seemed that way,
as we won the World Cup,
beating Germans 4-2 on the day

In 67, a famous speech by Wilson,
on the pound -
so with our currency de-valued,
our Economy's unsound

In 68 at Wembley,
Man U won the Euro bash -
it was a landmark win for Busby
just a decade from the crash

In 69, the Kray twins
sent to jail for thirty years,
although their mother Violet, was upset -
their foes shed little tears

1970 at the World Cup,
England's football team got beat,
so now, the country in a bad mood
brought a Labour Poll defeat

In 71, school children's milk
was axed, by Maggie Thatcher -
was a stupid act, that earned her nickname,
brazen "milk-snatcher"!

In 72, a Miners strike
and crisis - "three-day week" -
so Mr Heath went on the box
to tell us things weren't bleak

In 73, we joined the E E C
on New Years Day
and we also saw a "retail tax",
now V.A.T we'd pay

74, "Who Governs Britain?"
Heath's strange election shout -
the answer came - "Not you mate!"
- his Tories booted out.....

In 75, came Thatcher,
as she reached the Tory peak -
although not in charge of Britain YET,
that office she would seek.....

76 was very hot
of that, there is no doubt -
in fact, there was a ban on hosepipes
in the midst of summer drought

77, we're in the streets
for "Silver Jubilee" -
a quarter-century, she'd been Queen
her Royal Majesty!

78 - "Now sees the Winter
of our discontent" -
these strikes were country-wide, or so it seemed -
"We blame the Government!"

79 - the country's had enough,
it saw the light -
so the Tories regained power,
now the country's "Thatcherite"............

TO BE CONTINUED..........

"Ode to Winter" Wednesday January 6th 2010

"Go pour yourself a drop of gin, Jack Frost has come and snowed us in!".......

They say that global warming's rife, the facts are very clear -
one thing's for sure, as I can say that it's not ruddy here!
I hold a little scraper in my hand, I do not scoff -
so would the global know-alls like to scrape my windscreen off?
In short, it's blinkin' freezin' - weather for the Polar junkies -
my face is blue, my hands are too - it's Brass and Arctic monkeys!
Of course, I'm only joking cuz' I know what it's about -
the warm air in the South Pole pushes all the cold air out!
So then it reaches 'Blighty', bloody hell, oh thanks for that!
My thermo's showing minus six, an icy little stat!
I'm sick of winter weather now, I want the summer sun -
oh how I'd love to wear a t-shirt, how I crave the 'currant bun'!

The "Brass Monkey" and his balls

"Three Cheers for Mr Cabot"
Thursday January 7th 2010

"A well-known local pub chant that I heard being sung among the chaps in the 'London Inn' only last week"......

Three cheers for Mr Cabot!
And towers in his name!
To circumnavigate the globe
became his merry game!
Now when he got commissioned -
he cried "ooooo, bloody hell!
I'm sailing to the 'New World'
in a wooden caravel!"

"Hooray for Giovanni!"
(Italian for "John") -
and "All hail to Caboto -
thus to Bristol he has gone!"
Now this is what Venetians sang
as he left Italy
Then on he went, to England next -
to reach his destiny

Columbus was his rival
and to beat him would be heaven!
So John set out from Bristol -
in the spring of '97
Now all-onboard "The Matthew"
he sailed oceans far and wide -
and thus discovered *new found land* -
then took it in his stride

Now when I see the "Matthew"
I do think "Hallo there John!
It's been a good five hundred years
since you've been dead and gone!
But full of foreign tourists
I do see your bloody boat -
it goes up and down the Basin,
how it really gets my goat!

Round and round in circles,
not a voyage but a spin -
although you found America,
I wish they'd turn it in!
I applaud your great discoveries
of which they often speak -
But as for good ship "Matthew"
I do hope it springs a leak!"

"Peeps Diary - 1660-1669 (Fragments), by Sammy Peeps"
Saturday January 9th 2010

"Just a silly spoof really"......

Samuel Pepys - who by coincidence, also wrote a diary around this time

1/1/1660
My name henceforth is Sammy Peeps,
methinks I give myself the creeps -
the only persone in these tymes
who keeps a diary for his crymes!
My work by day is Navy Clerke,
I do find it a merrie larke
now Lizzie is my wife so deare
I hold her in a state of feare.
And so to bed.

1/6/1660
The country's Parliamentary Rump
has hit the ground with quite a bump,

now this can only mean one thing -
they want to re-appoint the King
Old Charlie boy's been gone ten years
and we ain't seen too many cheeres -
(a Royal Navy is the goal
for me to climb the greasy pole).
And so to bed.

3/1/1661
On checking my accounts did finde
my scrimping days are well behinde,
so I do live just like a Lord
and all the pleasures I afforde
Thank god that Cromwell's dead and gone -
now all the best plays are back on!
No longer living like a Monk -
I'm always out and roaring drunk!
And so to bed.

23/4/1661
Republique's up and on it's bike,
and Cromwell's head is on a pike
the Monarchy is back in place -
they'd kept a Charlie "Two" in case!
So there was much ado in towne
when "Young Pretender" got his crowne -
Could it be the Coronation
is a case of "On Probation"?
And so to bed.

7/6/1665
The Plague has come to our greate City!
An awful shame, oh such a pity!
Now every day, they shout "Oh ye! -
Bring oute your dead! Don't have to pay!
Don't even have to give a pounde
for us to stick 'em in the grounde -
If you've a Red Cross on your door
we'll know who's got the Plague for sure!"
With a certain sense of dreade - I a-go to bed.

2/9/1666
I saw a sight in towne last night -
olde London, it was all alight!
Had staggered home from whence the "Crowne"
no sooner in my dressing gowne
At 3am I was awoke -
to see our city all asmoke!
Upon this theme, I can't be vague -
(Although it may burn out the Plague?)
And so to bed.

4/9/1666
Forgot to say, the other night
that I was merrie, in a fight -
I found myself under a strain
and dropped cigar in Pudding Lane!
Now how it troubles conscience so -
to think of cockney tales of woe!

How many people have I slain?
Oh curses! For a lack of raine!
And so to bed.

2/3/1667
Nell Gwynn's an actress, oh so fair -
methinks I'd like to see her bare!
tis' whispered 'bout her underthings -
and how she loves to court the Kings!
Tis' also thought, King Charlie woos,
(an offer she might not refuse)
A scandal! If it made the news -
we'd hear a Royal round of boos!
And so, with that thought in my head -
I go to bed.

11/1/1668
Oh how my wifey blubbers so!
I'm not a big night-clubber though!
(But have a mistress on the side -
by name of Deb) - and we do hide
away, and play our naughty games
(while London town was up in flames)
Oh if my wife should ever spy
she'll hang my g---ies out to dry!
Much afeard - I go to bed.

4/6/1668

Last night with wifey I did supp,
we have seen fit to make it up -
and now we think it for the best -
to take a break and head out West
To Bath and Bristolle thus we go
for shopping, running to and fro -
to hell, I'll send my Navy larke
if it restrains my Missus barke!
And so to bed.

19-20/11/1668

There is a foul air aboute -
my wife has found my mistress out!
And she ran much "amok-ery"
by throwing all the crockery!
Now threatens her to burn my clothes
and slit my poor, fair Debbie's nose -
unless I give her twenty pound
so she'll leave home without a sound!
It is alas, with a sore head -
I go to bed.

31/5/1669

Wifey and me are pals at last,
now me and Debs are lovers past -
though could be that my failing eyes
will be a blessing in disguise!

The diary that I keep must cease,
my eyesight daily does decrease
I hope my journal is much-read -
alas, alack - I will be dead!
I bid farewell -
and go to bed.

THE END

"Manifesto of le comédie Party" - (by Carl Marks and Frederick Angels, 1848)
Sunday January 10th 2010

"From each according to their beads – to each according to their pleads"........

Karl Marx - who by coincidence, also stood for Communism

"There is a spectre haunting here,
the worker's day is drawing near -
Communism's home to roost
to give all working men a boost!

Methinks all men are born the same,
but Bourgeoisie have played a game -
my mate and I have worked it out
(that's Angels, fellow German lout)

We Communists express our views
in hope it will get on the news,
Now here's what me and Freddie found,
we think it will shock and astound (!) :-

In rare times of sobriety,
we found that in Society
the whole thing's been a big class fight -
' betwixt the mini and the might

Class struggles - there's a history,
(till now, it was a mystery) -
but now we know what it's about,
why, Fred and me will sort it out!

See how Borgeoisie misbehaves -
(they made us serfs, and plebs, and slaves!)
But now it's time to overthrow -
we think their wicked ways must go!

The Proletariat can't see
for far too long, it's not been free -
thank God that me and Fred are here
to make this scandal crystal clear!

Borgeoisie's heading for a fall,
the workers will be walking tall -
just like the storm the weather brings,
this is the natural way of things

Impatient thus to see them gone?
We've found a way to speed things on -
So shout 'em loud across the lands,
our list of Communist demands:-

1. Private lands we won't allow,
   it all goes Public, as of now -
...the greedy landlord's had his day -
...so no more rents for us to pay!

2. Your Income Tax is on the rise,
...we've looked at it, and think it wise -
...the workers will pay next to nowt,
...the richest get the biggest clout!

3. When you die, you can't leave cash
...so others profit in a flash -
...we'll teach your offspring not to bleat
...and learn to stand on their own feet

4. Emigrants, rebellious types -
...we trust that you will have no gripes,
...cuz' at the quickest diary date
...your "property", we'll confiscate

5. A National Bank for one and all,
...now that should prove a wake-up call -
...no private profits thrown about
...no bankers bonus to hand out

6. Transport will be Nationalised -
...Communication, centralised
...So thus will be their natural fate,
...it all goes back unto the State!

7. Take the factories - and production -
...bring all under State instruction
...so private industry's no more -
...Borgeoisie's got a shock in store!

8. Work for all! (That's if your fit)
...Cuz' everyone should do their bit -
...from each according to their means,
...to each according to their beans!

9. Take the role of Agriculture -
...mix it up with Manufacture
...divides 'twixt town and country go -
...to level population flow

10. Go tell every man and neighbour -
....we'll stop evil Child Labour!
....instead we'll have free educations
....for the children of our Nations!

This is how the worker gains,
they've nowt to lose, except their chains!
These are the Communist demands -
so working men in all the lands....................UNITE!!"

COPYRIGHT - Carl Marks and Frederick Angels, 1848.

EVENTUAL CONCLUSION OF MARKS (1867) -

"For my Great Work (without my pal),
you need to read "Der Kapital" -
for as you know, I have been led
where (Mr) Angels fears to tread!"

"On the Origin of Beasties (by Charlie Darwen, 1859)"
Monday January 11th 2010

"God's made a monkey out of us all!"........

Charles Darwin - who by coincidence, also discovered the "Origin of Species"

"Oh goodness me! It's hard to take -
The Holy Bible's big mistake!
I've just found out, my mouth's agape -
that man descended from the ape!
Methinks that Adam was a scam,
that Eve was pushed along in pram,
I don't think Noah had an Ark -
no cows to moo, no dogs to bark!

The thought of Eve from Adam's rib
had not done much for "Women's Lib" -
to men like me, they should give "Knights",
for sticking up for Ladies rights!

No serpent in that Garden fair,
no apple bites, no walking bare -
so Genesis cannot persist
with saying Eden DID exist!

You see, a-sailing I did go,
a-hunting high, a-hunting low,
the good ship "Beagle" took me forth
across the oceans, south and north
A lengthy voyage, quite a bore,
we ended up near Ecuador -
but found, just as we're getting cross
the islands of Galapagos

Oh goodness me! Great tortoise things!
They strut about, like Lords and Kings!
I'm not talking of reptiles such
you'd keep locked in your garden hutch!
To cut a lengthy story short,
found creatures of another sort -
they were great-great-great-great grandsons,
relations of the other ones!

And oh! To see those creatures swim!
I trust I'm not "out on a limb" -
and though it hurt to carry it,
I brought one back (called "Harriet")
Their story's been (though I loathe puns)
"survival of the fittest" ones
thus hit upon my new direction -
"Natural Theory of Selection"!

I know this will upset the church,
my vicar will give me the birch!
And goodness me - how will he cope (?) -
his Royal Holiness, The Pope!

But I refuse to hold my tongue,
I'll shout it with an iron lung -
"I do declare, though it's not funky -
Man descended from the monkey!"

"Leaders of Labour"   Friday January 22nd 2010

"Oh dear, oh dear, what awful luck – now Tony's gone and passed the buck!"........

There was a man called Tony Blair
he was all tooth and grin
..so single-mindedly he'd dare
......invade Iraq, and think it fair
.........ignored the protests, didn't care -
all arrogance and spin

He saw the storm was brewing
and thought that he'd step down
..finance did need reviewing -
......the bankers were mis-doing -
.........and unemployed were queuing -
"I'll hand to Gordon Brown"

There was a man called Gordon Brown
he was extremely bright
..But people didn't like his frown,
......they said "he's after Tony's crown,
..........most likely, bring the country down" -
the Public, they were right.......(?)

"Three Cheers for Billy Wedlock"
Monday January 25th 2010

(Birthday wishes to Billy)
A well-known local pub chant that was doing the rounds in the 'Hen and Chicken' only the other day"..........

Three cheers for Billy Wedlock!
and stands named after he -
The star of Bristol football
who was only five foot three!
Now despite his lack of inches
he would outjump all the rest -
more than twenty caps for England,
I'd say Billy was the best!

Hooray for Billy Wedlock!
and pubs named after he
(oh dear, they've knocked it down I note -
instead, it's R.I.P!)
A hundred years ago and more
he nearly won the Cup -
but Man United did make sure
that we were runners-up!

Now Billy-boy was not the type
of guy you'd go round kickin' -
cuz' he was "Bemmy" born and bred
(right by the "Hen and Chicken")
They called him "Fatty" Wedlock"
as he had a "little" belly -
But put a football at his feet
and he would give it welly!

Now when I'm sitting in his stand
I say "Hallo there Billy!
You were so good at heading balls,
you did it willy-nilly!"
But says the bloke who's next to me -
"You're mad - He won't reply -
the only place he's playing now
is right up in the sky!"

Page 122

"A text message" Saturday January 30th 2010

"Genuine text message, sent to a loved one when returning to Bristol from Weston-Super-Mare, after searching for poetry books. 30/01/10."

I have in my possession,
no book of Thomas Hood -
But G K Chesterton (I'm told)
is really just as good.

SO I GOT THAT INSTEAD.

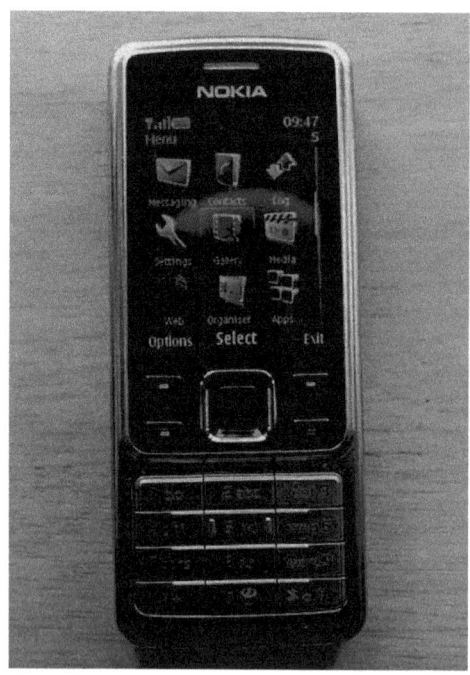

"The Cynic's Calender"   Sunday February 14th 2010

"The thing I really cannot take, is everybody's 'on the make' – to make a speedy profit's rife, in every aspect of our life.....
(A Valentine's rant – and well-known pub chant – given an airing at the 'Fox and Goose' only last week)".......

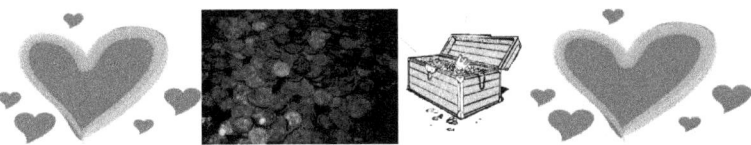

JANUARY
"We're 'Travel Agents PLC' - so book your holiday!
Christmas is now history, you'll want to go away!
Oh summertime, oh summertime, you'll be here in a flash,
so reserve your big vacation and just give us loads of cash!"

FEBRUARY
"We're 'Supermarkets PLC' - we want your money now!
Cuz if our profits don't go up this year, there's gonna be a row -
Oh Valentine, Oh Valentine, she how she rambles near -
we want a "Special" payday, every month of every year!"

MARCH
"We're British High Street leaders but the market's looking bleak,
so a quick return on our new line, in Spring, is what we seek -
Oh Mother's Day, oh Mother's Day, just see how close she comes,
now please give us some more profit in the name of all your mums!"

APRIL
"We're a former British chocolate firm who found a foreign buyer,
now the work has gone to Poland, leaving English in the mire -
Oh Easter time, oh Easter time, come quicker, Britain begs!
And Britons, please forgive us, cuz we need to sell our eggs!"

MAY (DAY)
"We're Britain's leading petrol firm, we'd like to give you thanks,
cuz we are the planet's "super-rich", (keep filling up your tanks!)
Bank Holiday, Bank Holiday, oh have a little drive -
(I bet you any money, you'll get stuck on the M5!")

JUNE
"We're your friendly High Street giants, and we're so misunderstood,
as our profits should be bigger, the position isn't good -
Oh Father's Day, oh Father's Day, see how that date advances -
now give us all your lolly to improve our circumstances!"

JULY
"We're 'Travel Agents PLC', (oh yes, we're back again!)
And we thought we'd better let you know, last-minute deals for Spain
Now come on folks, don't miss the boat, you know that it makes sense,
cuz' you need a sunny fortnight, so don't sit upon the fence!"

AUGUST
"We're your corporate supermarket chain - we are in such a mess!
Cuz the Public's gone on holiday, our goods are selling less -
Oh Christmas time, oh Christmas time, you seem so far away -
we long for your festivities, it brings us bonus pay!"

SEPTEMBER
"We're motor manufacturers, (please buy a Ford or Rover)
and our newest cars have come in on the Ferry (via Dover)
Now give us all your savings on the first September date,
so then you'll get a gleaming motor with the very newest plate!"

OCTOBER
"We are your local Pound Shop and we need an Autumn date,
cuz *witch*-ever way you look at it, our cashflow's in a state -
Oh Halloween, oh Halloween, your coming is a sign,
cuz' we need a little windfall that will boost our "bottom-line"

NOVEMBER
"We're your local, handy corner-store - our shoppers get their perks,
now we've got a rather decent line in cheapy fireworks -
Oh Bonfire, Oh Bonfire, at long last, you arrive -
oh thank god for Mr Guy Fawkes in the year 1605!"

DECEMBER
Jingle bells, oh Jingle bells! oh, how the months do fly,
you're our very favourite time of year, it's money from the sky!
Oh Christmas Time, oh Christmas Time, we're rolling in the dough -
so thank god for baby Jesus, who was born so long ago!"

"Holly"   Monday February 15th 2010

"Domestic troubles"..........

I've never known a little dog
that needs so much attention -
the tickles I must give this hound,
too numerous to mention

I wish the mutt would leave me be,
go sit upon the stair -
instead of lying on it's back,
four legs up in the air........

"TV Scams of the 21st Century"
Friday February 19th 2010

"Ring us now, cuz' times are lean – there's 'Talent' on your TV screen!"........

Part One - The Age of the Talent "Elimination" Show

Thought some bright spark at ITV,
"we're in a fix, now let me see -
how can I raise some ready cash
to stop TV's financial crash?"

"a-ha! I've got the very thing!
let's find young people who can sing -
who want to get their lifelong dream
(for us, a money-making scheme!)"

"We'll get some mugs to sing a song,
at home, the viewers play along -
reject contestants as they please -
(by phone) - then we'll collect the fees"

"By charging them for each phone-call,
we'll rake it in, we'll have a ball -
our fortunes have been on the slide,
but play this right - we'll turn the tide"

"It could be like the BBC,
an unofficial, mini fee -
this does seem like the way to go
in order to increase cash-flow"

So after bosses were consented,
thus a programme was invented -
a judging panel put in place,
but viewers would dictate the race

The BBC did watch in awe,
they knew it did not break the law
and thought the chance too good to miss -
"Now *WE* will have a bit of this!"

When *"Popstars"* finished on TV,
the Beeb had *"Fame Academy"*,
then was invented "*Pop Idol*"
with Simon Cowell "know-it-all"

"*X Factor*" was the next to run
(the biggest thing under the sun) -
although it had a different name,
"*Pop Idol*" had been just the same!

Now Cowell, he was all the rage
(concerning his "*X Factor*" wage -
the rumours they were running rife,
he was, for sure, set up for life.....)

Now these shows were a big success,
and viewing figures did impress -
though BBC had yet to find
the right reply, they were behind

So they would solve the mystery
by going back in history -
reviving an old dancing show
(re-titled, starting "*Strictly*" though)

Old codger Forsyth was dragged out
to compere this annoying bout
of ballroom dancing knockout show
where stars were told "Dance well - or GO!"

The "other side" thought this was nice
so they brought us "*Dancing on Ice*"
(and just for those with iron wills,
Beeb's just announced "*Dancing on Wheels*" !!)

So dancing on the BBC
and singing on the ITV,
then ice-skating was set to reign -
you think that's it (?) - then think again!

Now not content with "*Idol*" pay
(exporting it to USA),
the format had not over-ran -
so Simon hatched another plan......

This Cowell, he would not relent -
he wanted "*Britain's got Talent*"
(the show would make a singing "Royal"
of lumpy-dumpy Susan Boyle)

These programmes were all much the same,
identical, in all but name -
the same old scripts from show to show
the sound-bytes we would get to know

Competing egos on a Panel
whatever show, whichever channel,
their jobs to judge, make comments rude -
like Pantomime, the audience booed

(Contestant):- "*Vote to keep me IN -
my one big wish is that I'll win,
so help me to achieve my dream........*"
- this was the over-echoed theme

Presenters had repeated whines
(rehearsing complicated lines -
this was not needed, came down to -
"*So who goes now, it's down to YOU!*") #

Now whilst the twinkle-toes got dancing,
Public votes brought cash advancing -
TV screens awash with singing,
cash-tills, they did go a-ringing.........

These programmes are still round today
(monopolies won't go away) -
THAT phrase is all I seem to hear,
it's ever drummed into my ear

The bandwagon's still running loose,
the Nation's head is in a noose -
"Idol" / "Dancing" / "Talent" - all -
there's been a bloody bucketful

By time you've voted like a geek,
on EVERY show on, EVERY week -
you have incurred a spending spree -
a voluntary "licence fee".......

So just how did it come to this?
the "Ring-athon" does take the p---,
it seems they just want us to spend
on phone calls (which they do depend)

When talking of this TV con,
I must say "Where's the money gone?"
Which leads me on now to reflect
upon another sad subject –

Part Two - The Scam of the TV phone-in Quiz

Now what did TV channels do
before the "phone-in" quiz?
Where did they get their money from
until this dubious swiz?

How dare they patronise us so,
we're not incompetents -
insulting questions for the thick,
with no intelligence

*"Please call us now - A, B or C -
Just ring to win the prize.
There are two stupid answers there -
the "normal" one applies"*

*"Not trying to say you're dumb you see
It's just that we need cash
so we've put two silly options in
to profit in a flash"*

Who WAS a famous Beatle?
Was it Winston, Jane or John?
And name this film - "BLANK with the Wind" -
"Blowing" "Back" or "Gone" ?

Who was a TV weatherman?
"Seaweed" "Crab" or "Fish"?
"Chop Suey" is a Chinese WHAT?
"Proverb" "Man" or "Dish" ?

"So ring us now, we need your call -
can't have our phone-lines dead
We make our answers easy
cuz we're millions in the red".

"I blame the Government!" Tuesday February 23rd 2010

"The strange things one hears being said as you go about your daily life"..........

"The River Avon's burst it's banks, there's water in the street -
I've walked that dog across the fields, now I've got soaking feet!
It must be all that rain we've had, they never get it right -
they said there would be sunny spells, the weather would be bright!
Now we all know whose fault this is, *they're* so imcompetant,
let's start up a petition quick -
"I blame the Government!"

The paper's not arrived again, and neither has the post -
oh, Im fed up with complaining now, I've given up the ghost!
There's nothing on my TV screen, the schedule is a joke -
I've only got four channels cuz' the Digibox is broke!
Now we all know whose fault this is, *they* are so ignorant,
let's head off down to Parliament -
"I blame the Government!"

I queued up for the bus today, then couldn't get a seat -
it's happened every day this week, the problem does repeat!
There's roadworks everywhere you look, they're always digging holes!
Yet what it's for, god only knows - the Council's concrete moles!
Now we all know whose fault this is, the facts are evident -
so get your letters in the post,
"I blame the Government!"

Those traffic lights don't seem to work, they're always stuck on 'red'!
Yet Council Tax is up again, I swear we're being bled!
Another queue in Sainsbury's, yet half the till's don't run -
so is it any wonder we can't get our shopping done?
Now we all know whose fault this is, but *they're* not permanent -
so get off down the Council House,
"I blame the Government!"

I tried to find a garage, but there's barely *one* in town -
and then I had to queue *again*, and prices don't go down!
That fox has been again last night, and going through my bin -
all strewn across the pavement, I do think that it's a sin!
Now we all know whose fault this is, they are so insolent -
let's show 'em we won't stand for it,
"I blame the Government!"

My computer's slowed right down again, it *should* be going *fast*!
A "Techno Revolution"? Oh, I knew it wouldn't last!
The "Digital Economy"? They said it with a smirk!
My Broadband's lost connection and my ruddy mouse won't work!
Now we all know whose fault this is, their fall is imminent -
let's show 'em at the Polling Booth,
"I blame the Government!"

The cost of milk's gone up again and bread is *never* cheap!
Prices high, but we are broke - Recession's cutting deep!
In short, the country's in a mess - I'd sell up if I could -
oh, modern life is rubbish and the future isn't good!
Now we all know whose fault this is, 'cuz we're intelligent -
so vote the buggers out in May -
"I BLAME THE GOVERNMENT!!"

"A Five-Point Manifesto" (AKA 'A Personal Pipedream')
Tuesday March 2nd 2010

"What it says on the tin............"

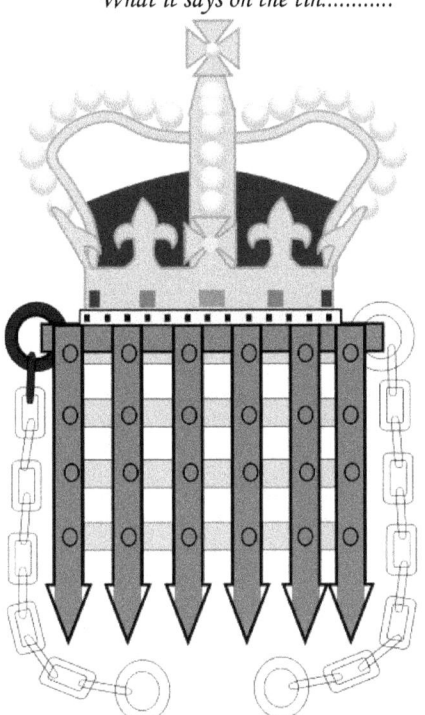

Part One – On Royalty and Aristocracy

Let's tax the rich to help the poor –
the Upper classes must pay more
so close the gap in poverty
to benefit Society

To take the crown of Royalty,
let's do away with Monarchy –
for *UN*-elected 'Heads of State"
no money to accommodate

Re-open houses of high classes
to benefit the working masses,
who then could visit, pay a fee
and wallow in past history

To safeguard Royal Industry
don't need an actual family –
their stately homes and lands remain
to generate financial gain.......

Part Two – On Lottery and Health #

Divert the National Lottery wealth
and put it into National Health
there isn't a more 'worthy cause',
a noble plan with no real flaws

For every single ticket bought
the wasted funds would total 'nought',
perhaps let every player choose –
'Cash to the Arts, or cut the queues?'

The Lottery is a waste of time,
they chuck the cash, so it's a crime
Now "waste not, want not's" what I say –
let's put it into Health today!

When 'Camelot' has had it's day,
then nationalizing is the way –
the Lottery would belong to us,
without the Corporation fuss

Part Three – On Crime, Drugs and Class

The reasons crime exist are clear
but just in case, I'll re-state here –
Cause One is envy, gulfs in class.....
Cause Two is drugs, supplied *en-masse*

You cut the drugs, you cut the crime –
you cut supplies, and jail the slime,
a fine's no good, let's build more jails –
without 'life terms', so justice fails.....

Now coming back to gulfs in class,
to wanton envy, 'lack of brass',
we need some wealth re-distribution –
"Tax the rich in retribution!"

Divisions in Society
will lead to crime, it's plain to see –
youth boredom, inactivity
breeds budding criminality

Now 'Envy' is a great emotion,
(breeds 'material' devotion) –
the Upper classes roll in it,
hence workers want a little bit!

I've said, through Tax and Monarchy
let's trim the Aristocracy,
as merging 'class' in all good time
will lead to massive falls in crime

In short, the way this country's split
(the class and wealth divides in it) –
it's pretty much the very pills
responsible for Britain's ills......

Part Four – A "Robin Hood" or Tobin Tax ##

There is a global tax proposed
on bankers, it would be imposed –
it's in the name of 'Robin Hood'
and 'robs' the rich for common good

See, billions switched between the banks
(and massive corporation tanks) –
these deals at present, are tax-free,
which is a *slight* anomaly!

Currency Exchange and such,
plus stocks and bonds too, just as much –
these are the things that currently
the banks can swap without a "fee"

Now through a careful calculation
(not mere idle speculation) –
banks would pay a fraction more
in order to relieve the poor

cuz' from well under *one percent*
of these transactions would cement
and generate a huge amount –
a bigger sum than I can count!

Now, Bankers wouldn't feel the pinch,
their tiny loss would be a cinch –
just 50p in every "Grand"
is hardly an unfair demand!

And as I said, you'd be amazed
at sums of cash that would be raised –
now *every* Nation could expect
sheer *billions* used to resurrect.....

That's 2-5-0 in billion pounds
in which to do the global rounds –
(the estimated sums per year
in which to bring the world some cheer)

Half of which would be relayed
to climate change and foreign aid –
the other half on home affairs
like NHS, and social cares

Imagine if ten Nations signed,
all with a global tax in mind –
that's 25 in billions to
our Treasury to spend anew

Our share in tens of billions, see –
straight into *our* Economy,
in which to cut our National debts
and pour into our prize assets

Imagine all that extra wealth
all going on our National Health –
or billions put into our schools,
or prisons for our guilty fools!

All whilst knowing that we've set
the other half on foreign debt –
that's money spent to help the poor –
and tackle climate change the more

So I'm supporting 'Robin Hood',
which can but just, result in good –
I think we need a Banker's Tax,
which currently, the system lacks

Part Five – Re-nationalizing the Industries

Bring them back to Public care,
for *us* to run and *us* to share –
The "Public" Industries I mean,
the country would be very keen

Too long under "Private" attack,
these businessmen should get the sack –
the railway lines would be a start,
the Lottery would be pretty smart

They have been run for private gain
where profit's been the issue main –
the theme is greed, without a doubt,
these bonuses all thrown about!

It's *not* the share price on the climb -
let's aim to get the trains on time!
It's *not* your corporate designs -
let's have some decent railway lines!

They *should* be run with little fuss,
accountable to only *US!*
So shout it loud across the lands –
and bring 'em back to Public hands!

OVERVIEW

Trimming Aristocracy,
through Tax and ousting Monarchy
and ploughing National Lottery wealth
straight into funds for National Health

Whilst building prisons for the slime,
cuz' drug dealers must do their time,
and benefit Society
by closing gaps in poverty

A tax on banks, through 'Robin Hood'
to 'rob' the rich for common good –
and industries re-nationalized,
in other words, *un*-privatized

And one more thing – forgot to say
(more details on another day) –
asylum-seekers should remain,
as long as Britain feels the gain

A programme for equality,
for fairness in society –
re-distribution of the wealth
is just the thing for Britain's health

So this is all I have to say
until another rainy day –
I'd implement this if I could
And if I was PM, I would!......

"The Ticking Clock"   Monday March 8th 2010

"To a gutless fraud"..........

See how the clock does tick with time
and pretty soon, that clock will chime,
now this will mean your judgment date -
by then, it will be much too late...........

"Ode to the Sun"   Sunday March 28th 2010

"You can shine on me all day, but will the Earth be here to stay?"

Hello, good morning, you are out - hip-hip, hip-hip - hooray!!
Let's hope you're here to stay with us, let's hope you're here all day!
Enough of these festivities, a question, if I may -
they tell me we've a struggle on to keep yourself at bay!
Now is it true that human actions pay a heavy price?
I've heard you're over-heating us and melting all our ice!
So if we've made a little hole in Mr Ozone's layer -
it may be that we've lost all hope, we haven't got a prayer!
Pray tell me 'fore I rest my head, before I go to bed -
I want to know your answer to this thing that I have said
So, yes it's nice to see you and I'm glad you make me brown -
but tell me 'fore you go tonight, before you settle down.........

"Ode to the Moon"   Monday March 29th 2010

"A luny tune".......

Oh thou moon, your day is gone - no longer something new -
the Poets sing your praise no more, since Armstrong conquered you
Although I grab my telescope and view you every night,
'tis not the same whilst knowing you've been reached by NASA flight!
That's not to say that I'd turn down the chance to walk on you -
but then, I know I'll never be part of Apollo's crew
So truth be told, to look at you, I'm really not too fussed -
It's just that I don't want my instruments collecting dust!
Oh moon, you are okay but then, when all is done and said -
a minutes view's enough for me, then time I got in bed.......

"Twentieth Century Britain (Part Five)"   Thursday April 1st 2010

"Oh dear, it's April 1st"............

......*April Fools!!!*

"All on April Fool's Day"
Thursday April 1st 2010

"For Paula Anne Williams".......

Prince Otto Bismarck - he was born
an April Fool, that's on my life!
And so was David Gower too -
and so was Churchill's wife

Rachmaninov - not born in May,
but April 1st, like Chaney *
Whoever said that day brought fools
was clearly none too brainy

Hold on a mo - I'll take that back
(Research did go astray)
Chris Evans - famous fool DJ -
he too was born that day!

"Small Faces" Ronnie Lane as well
(I couldn't find a Royal) -
merely actress Ms MacGraw
and singer Susan Boyle

English were the fools one year,
way back, when times were lean -
through losing Berwick to the Scots -
AD 1318

Skip forward now, six hundred years,
the "Great War" we had seen
Two bodies merged, that formed the R A F - **
(nineteen - eighteen)

In '24, we saw that scoundrel Hitler
sent to jail
Once there, he'd write a foolish book,
("Mein Kampf") - then out on bail

Now what of the Americans,
when in the "Second" War?
They bombed the Swiss - by accident -
in 1944

In '48, food and supplies
dropped in on East Berlin, ***
then later, Russians built a wall -
"KEEP TROUBLE-MAKERS IN!"

The "Irish Free State" was re-named -
AGAIN - in '49,
they called it the "Republic" ****
then decided that was fine

In '57, the greatest April Fool hoax,
on TV -
It made us think there was such thing
as a "Spaghetti Tree"! *****

Now Maggie Thatcher's "Poll-tax"
hit the Scots first, '89 -
but true to form, when asked to pay -
that Nation would decline......

Now Marvin Gaye, in '84,
was gunned down by his Dad
And Strangeways started rioting - ******
it's prisoners, raving mad!

Don't believe me? Check those history books
(which were my tools)
But all these things DID happen
on the day of April Fools!

NOTES:-

* *U S actor Alonso "Lon" Chaney*
** *The two bodies were the Royal Naval Air Service and the Royal Flying Corps*
*** *The "Berlin Airlift"*
**** *"Republic of Ireland"*
***** *On BBC's "Panorama" programme*
****** *Strangeways Prison riot, 1990.*

C.A.T.A.S.T.R.O.P.H.E.   Friday April 16th 2010

"I couldn't think up an acronym for C.A.T.A.S.T.R.O.P.H.E. Still, it's a good title thought, isn't it?

Cats are in her flat
cats are on her mat
cats are in a spat
cats are getting fat,
Cats are in her head
cats are being fed
cats are being bred
cats are in her shed
...............they're even in her bed!
Cats are on her brain
cats are up her drain
cats have left a stain
(cats are such a pain!)
Cats are in the street
cats are at her feet
cats are on her sheet
cats are eating meat
...............they're eating 'Shredded Wheat'!
Cats are being bad
cats are going mad
cats do make her glad -
they're in her sketching pad!

Cats are showing flaws
cats are showing claws
cats are breaking laws -
cats are such a nause!
..................they're even watching 'Jaws'!
Cats are in her lair
cats are shedding hair
cats are in her glare -
cats are on the stair!
Cats are on her path
cats are in her bath,
they're sat on Aunty Kath -
they're never in her wrath!
Cats are at her door
cats are on the floor
cats are in her drawer -
cats are such a chore!
Cats are on her lap
cats are in a scrap,
cats under the tap!
They never take a nap!
Cats are in her Jag
cats are in her bag
cats are in her mag' -
but cats are such a drag!
Cats are in her bog
cats are sat agog
cats are in her blog!
cats are out in fog -
.............and chasing next door's dog!
Cats are in her kitchen
cats are all a twitchin'
cats have got her itchin'
cats are so bewitchin'!
Cats are sitting purring
cats are sat de-furring
cats are self-injuring,
cats are debt-incurring!
cats are not enduring!!

So why, **why, why??**

"A week to go before the Election"
Thursday April 29th 2010

"God's punishment on the Nation?"

..........and God did say he'd send a scourge,
a pestilence would thus emerge -
so if you think we've had it bad,
you *will* cry out for what we *had!*

When plagues of locusts sweep the land,
like Robin and his merry band -
yet in reverse, they'll rob the poor
to feed their cronies all the more!

There is this candidate I know
who says and does things all for show -
He is the smiling, public face
who represents his Party's case

But we all know what's going on,
it's really just a massive con -
"forget my wealth, your votes I crave -
I *am* a toff, but 'call me Dave'!"

Now when he's visiting a school,
he'll try and make himself look cool -
his jacket will not satisfy,
so *it* comes off, as will his tie

The fact he was an 'Eton pup',
his Party's tried to cover up -
silver-spooned from pram to grave,
"but don't mind that, just 'call me Dave'!"

What has the country gone and done?
Life *used* to be so full of fun -
but now we've got an Eton ponce
as Tory cronies Blair response

"New Labour's" going in the bin,
it seems we've got Tone's Tory twin -
"Now as PM, I will behave,
forget my school, and 'call me Dave'!"

........"and God did say he'd send a scourge,
a pestilence would thus emerge -
so if you think we've had it bad............................

??

???

"..............oh my god, a grinning cad!!!!"

"Famous last thoughts (?)" Friday April 30th 2010

"His life did flash before him........and gave him chance to think......... 'so have I led a useful life – or did I cause a stink?'"...........

Captain John Smith had a bad thought
when the iceberg struck "Titanic" -
"I've left the light on at my house -
oh god, I'm in a panic!"

Thought Hitler (gun in mouth)
when in his den under Berlin -
"Did Eva take those extra pills,
or throw them in her bin?"

Thought JFK in motorcade,
in Dallas, after brunch -
"I am still feeling peckish,
now I wonder what's for lunch?"

Thought Captain Oates, when off for evening stroll,
out in the snow -
"Bugger this, 'Go back!' -
that chicken soup is on the go!"

Thought Isambard Kingdom Brunel
sat on the lavatory -
"Oh god, I've left my lunchbox
up the Downs 'Obervatory'!"

Thought Mussolini (with his wife)
still in his dressing gown -
"I've always had this blasted fear
of hanging upside down!"

Thought good old Mr Lincoln
at the theatre, '65 -
"Good lord, this play is life-like,
I'm so glad to be alive!"

Thought Charlie First, our noble King -
all set to get the chop -
"Thank god I've had a haircut,
'cuz my head's about to drop!"

Thought Joan of Arc, all set to burn
and feeling rather bold -
"I do wish they'd get on with it,
I'm feeling rather cold!"

Thought Chairman Mao, of China,
with his goose about to cook -
"I've never even read a copy
of my own 'Red Book'!"

Thought Elvis Aaron Presley,
looking good at 42 -
"I've had that extra burger,
now I think I need the loo!"

Thought good old Viscount Nelson,
just about to meet his death -
"I wish you hadn't kissed me, Hardy –
you've got stinky breath!"

Thought mighty Julius Caesar
just before he hit the ground -
"Thank god I've got my greatest mates
here with me, gathered round!"

Final thought:-

*Thought our Lord God in heaven,
after this world, he did make -
"I sometimes think I might have made
a terrible mistake!"........................*

PHOTOS AND ILLUSTRATIONS

All photos and illustrations (except where indicated*) are copyright-free, and from the Wikimedia Commons website.

commons.wikimedia.org

Main cover sleeve image "Clifton Suspension Bridge" by Hariprasath Raajaraajan
Back cover sleeve image "Smoking balloon (Mongolfier brothers')" by Unknown
First inner page image, "Clifton Suspension Bridge" from *"Bristol Past and Present"*
Image from "Foreward" – "Angry man (Profanity)" by Tomia.

1. Images from "The Good old days" – "Queen Square riots, Bristol, 1831" from *"Bristol Past and Present"*. "Plague" by Unknown.
2. Images from "Three cheers for Mr Colston" – "Edward Colston" by Unknown. "Colston's School" from *"Bristol Past and Present"*.
3. Image from "Our Noble Family" – "Badge of the Royal House of Windsor" by Sodacan
4. Images from "Our Noble Leader" – "Gordon Brown" by IMF, "New Labour-style rose" by Peggy Greb.
5. Image from "The Celebrity Chef" - "Gordon Ramsay" by jo-h.
6. Images from "26-5-1999 (Two minutes of torture)" – "European Cup" by Riccardo de conciliis, "Man United kit" by Victor baron.
7. Image from "The world's a giant car-park" – "Traffic jam" by Jürgen Ludwig
8. Image from "Twentieth Century Britain (Part One)" – "Queen Victoria" by W. and D. Downey
9. Image from "The man in the stove-pipe hat" – "Brunel" by Unknown
10. Images from "Paradise Glossed" – "Love hearts" by FML. "Bush and Blair" by Eric Draper.
11. Image from "The Asda Trilogy" – "Asda (Keighley)" by Mtaylor848
12. Images from "25-5-2005 (Six minutes of ecstacy)" – European Cup by Riccardo de conciliis, Liverpool kit by Felato.
13. Image from "If I was born in 1937" – "Labour Election poster 1945" by Parti Labour
14. Image from "The Politician who told the truth" – "The Politician (The Subsidised Mineowner)" by Unknown.
15. Image from "Twentieth Century Britain (Part Two)" – "Airship 101" by Unknown
16. Images from "Three cheers for Mr Plimsoll" – "Samuel Plimsoll I" by Unknown. "Samuel Plimsoll II" by J. Nash
17. Images from "B.I.G.B.A.L.L.s. (or 'The Great Balloon Hunt')" – "Smoking balloon (Mongolfier brothers')" by Unknown, "Spherical balloon" + "Brint balloon 1783" also both by Unknown, "Big Balloon" (Luftschiff Montgolfier) by Brockhaus Konversations-Lexikon
18. Image from "Local news is rubbish" – "Bedminster Mural" by Geof Sheppard
19. Image from "I am a child of Thatcher" – Margaret Thatcher" by Steve Punter

20. Images from "Evolution of the telephone" – "1896 telephone" by Unknown. "Mobile phone evolution" by Marus.
21. Images from "The Scotsman's day out in Bristol" – "Avon Gorge and Clifton Suspension Bridge (1879)" by Unknown. "Scotsman balloon" by Ruth Ellison
22. Image from "Twentieth Century Britain (Part Three)" – "Dunkirk Evacuation" by Inconnu.
23. Image from "Ode to Autumn"- "Autumn leaves" by Augustine Lim
24. Images from "P.C. Cobb (Who had a hard job)" – "Policeman at traffic light" by Klaus D Peter AKA Enigma51. "Policeman II" by the George Eastman Collection.
25. Image from "Accents, according to the media" – "Air traffic controller" by Mark Brouwer
26. Image from "The Daily Redtop" – "Foreign man with tabloid newspaper" by Once burst2
27. Image from "The Spirit of Women's Rights" – "Christobel Pankhurst and Suffragettes" – by Johnny Cyprus.
28. Image from "Deals on meals" – "Burgers and chips" by Jess Sawrey
29. Image from "Loud ugly chap" - "Silhouette of a man" by Liftarn
30. Image from "Paper Man" – "Ghostly image of man reading paper on a bench" – by Asio otus
31. Image from "The Zzzzz Factor" – "Microphone" by Zzubnik
32. Image from "Early Morning" – "Victoria Park, Bedminster" by Martin Clark.
33. Image from "The Tenth Doctor Who" – "Doctor Who (David Tennant)" by "Doctor Who 2009 The Waters of Mars Footage 5.ogv (User ahremsee) – Modifications by Cirt.
34. Image from "Doctor Blinker" – "Doctor examination" by Klaus D Peter AKA Enigma51.
35. Images from "Twentieth Century Britain (Part Four)" – "Harold Wilson" by PHC Harold Wise. "Edward Heath" by Frank Hall.
36. Images from "Ode to Winter" – "Wintry scene" by Hans Baluschek. "Brass Monkey and his balls" by Vmenkov
37. Image from "Three cheers for Mr Cabot" – "John Cabot/Giovanni Caboto" by Unknown.
38. Image from "Peeps Diary - 1660-1669 (Fragments), by Sammy Peeps" – "Samuel Pepys" by John Hayls.
39. Image from "Manifesto of le comédie Party" - (by Carl Marks and Frederick Angels, 1848) – "Karl Marx" from the University of Texas, Austin.
40. Images from "On the Origin of Beasties (by Charlie Darwen, 1859)" – "Charles Darwin ape with monkey and mirror" by **Faustin Betbeder**. "**Charles Darwin** large ape image" by Unknown
41. Images from "Leaders of Labour" – "Tony Blair caricature" by **Strassengalerie** . "Gordon Brown caricature" by Edward Drantler
42. Image from "Three cheers for Billy Wedlock" – "Wedlock Stand, Ashton Gate, Bristol City FC" by Matt101
43. Image from "A text message" – "Nokia Mobile phone" by Racklever.
44. Images from "The Cynic's Calender" – "Love hearts" by FML. "Gold coins" by Swiss Banker. "Treasure chest" by The Evil Spartan.
45. *Image from "Holly" – "Holly the dog" (from author's Private Collection) – by John Davies.
46. Images from "TV scams of the 21st Century" – "Silver mobile phone" by *Andrew Fitzsimon*. *"Microphone"* by Nicolas Esposito

47. Image from "I blame the Government!" - "Angry man (Profanity)" by Tomia.
48. Image from "A Five-Point Manifesto" (A.K.A. 'A Personal Pipedream') – "Portcullis (Somerset Herald Badge)" by Ipankonin
49. Image from "The ticking clock" – "Clock" by Andreas Praefcke
50. Image from "Ode to the Sun" – "The Sun" ("Paradiso Canto") from *'The Divine Comedy by Dante',* illustrated by Gustave Doré
51. Image from "Ode to the Moon" – "Map of the moon" by Johannes Hevelius
52. Images from "Twentieth Century Britain (Part Five)" - "Big Balloon" (Luftschiff Montgolfier) by Brockhaus Konversations-Lexikon. "April Fools Postcards" by Unknown.
53. Image from "All on April Fool's Day" – Mischievous little girl" by Luigi Crosio
54. Images from C.A.T.A.S.T.R.O.P.H.E"- "Mischievous cats" by Henriëtte Ronner – Knip. "Miseries of human life – Cat-sitting", engraving by Isaac Cruikshank after a drawing by Woodward
55. Images from "A week to go before the Election" – "God appearing through the clouds" (*"Die Bibel in Bildern"*) by Julius Schnorr von Carolsfeld. "Arrow symbol" by Pearson Scott Foresman. "David Cameron" by Land of Hope and Glory.
56. Images from "Famous last thoughts (?)" – "Adolf Hitler" by Slime Turtle. "Benito Mussolini" by Muzej Revolucije Narodnosti Jugoslavije. "Abraham Lincoln" by D. Van Nostrand. "Julius Caesar" by Amadscientist ".
"The Voyage of Life – Old Age" by Thomas Cole.

ALL COVER SLEEVE IMAGES HAVE BEEN REFERRED TO IN THE ABOVE LIST.

Web-links for the *"A Five-Point Manifesto"* poem:-

#

http://www.facebook.com/profile.php?id=1303050646#!/notes/national- lottery-cash-for-the-nhs/the-plan-/273161127298

##
http://www.facebook.com/profile.php?id=1303050646#!/robinhoodtax?ref=ts

http://robinhoodtax.org.uk/

http://www.waronwant.org/

http://www2.labour.org.uk/home

At the time of going to press...........

"Fingers crossed, and hold your nose
cuz' where we're going, no-one knows......
now Britain's landed in the dung -
the Parliamentary House is 'hung'
Will Davy do a deal with Nick?
The very thought does make me sick!
Or Clegg is shaking Gordon's hand?
- to keep them masters of the land...........

Fingers crossed, and hold your breath
we're going on a dance of death –
I hope and will with all I've got
The Liberals back the Labour lot..........

FAT CHANCE!!

To be continued – so watch this space.....

www.ingramcontent.com/pod-product-compliance
Ingram Content Group UK Ltd.
Pitfield, Milton Keynes, MK11 3LW, UK
UKHW021320180426
11947UKWH00015B/1339